Developing

Diversity

In Organizations

A Digest of Selected Literature

Developing

Diversity

In Organizations

A Digest of Selected Literature

Ann M. Morrison
Kristen M. Crabtree

Center for Creative Leadership
Post Office Box 26300
Greensboro, North Carolina 27438-6300

The Center for Creative Leadership is an international, nonprofit educational institution founded in 1970 to foster creative leadership and effective management for the good of society overall. As a part of this mission, it publishes books and reports that aim to contribute to a general process of inquiry and understanding in which ideas related to leadership are raised, exchanged, and evaluated. The ideas presented in its publications are those of the author or authors.

The Center thanks you for supporting its work through the purchase of this volume. If you have comments, suggestions, or questions about any Center publication, please contact Bill Drath, Publication Director, at the address given below.

Center for Creative Leadership
Post Office Box 26300
Greensboro, North Carolina 27438-6300

©1993 Center for Creative Leadership
All rights reserved
Printed in the United States of America

ISBN 0-912879-70-X
Library of Congress Catalog Card Number: 93-44970
CCL No. 317

General Contents

Complete Contents

Acknowledgements

We are grateful for the support of the Center for Creative Leadership and the many staff members who helped us with this digest. We especially appreciate the assistance of the Center's library staff—Peggy Cartner, Frank Freeman, and Carol Keck—in identifying and obtaining references on diversity that were used for this digest and for other projects over the years.

Several researchers and trainers at the Center were instrumental in helping us select and evaluate references. Rick Morales and Marian Ruderman served as reviewers through both parts of the review process (described in the Introduction), and Lily Kelly reviewed during the first stage.

Four outside reviewers also contributed considerable time and expertise to this venture. Donna Thompson of Baruch College, the City University of New York, spent many hours of her summer leave reviewing our latest list and descriptions, providing additional references, and advising us on final content. Kay Iwata of Pacific Resources Education Programs in San Francisco served as a reviewer through the entire process. Taylor Cox at the University of Michigan Business School and Danelle Scarborough with the City of San Diego's Organizational Effectiveness Department were also reviewers through the first stage. In addition, Bernardo Ferdman of the State University of New York at Albany advised us on additional references to include.

We received valuable editorial assistance from several Center staff members—Bill Drath, Marcia Horowitz, and Martin Wilcox—and administrative support from Marlene Zagon.

These individuals and the Center have made this project possible and have made this final version much stronger than what we could have achieved on our own.

Introduction

This digest contains descriptions and analyses of articles and books that we believe are the most helpful for organizational leaders, human resource managers, and consultants in developing diversity in an organization.

The eighty-five works cited here are organized according to the five-step action process, derived from Guidelines on Leadership Diversity research and described in Morrison's *The New Leaders: Guidelines on Leadership Diversity in America* (Jossey-Bass, 1992). This research describes a variety of "best practices" that organizations can use to foster diversity. The five action steps constitute practical guidelines that managers need to assess an organization's diversity needs, design customized programs, and measure results.

The five steps are:

Step 1: Discover (and Rediscover) Diversity Problems in Your Organization.

Step 2: Strengthen Top-Management Commitment.

Step 3: Choose Solutions That Fit a Balanced Strategy.

Step 4: Demand Results and Revisit Goals.

Step 5: Use Building Blocks to Maintain Momentum.

These steps are described in further detail at the beginning of their respective sections.

How to Use This Digest

The descriptions of references are organized into six main categories: the five action steps described in *The New Leaders* and a small selection of general references. Within each category, references are sequenced in alphabetical order by the first author's last name and are further separated by specific topics. Step 3 on selecting diversity practices, for example, has sections on "Recruitment," "Development" (with subsections on "Mentoring" and "Awareness Training"), and "Accountability." Readers interested in work presented at recent conferences or other reports available only from the author may turn to the Appendix which lists a few of these references, including access information.

Readers interested in learning more about a particular step in the process of developing diversity may use the General Contents to turn first to that step, or to a section of that step. They can also get an overview of what is included in this digest or to see where a particular reference has been categorized and described by turning to the Complete Contents. To find a listing of all of the authors of selections described in this book, readers are referred to the Index at the end of this book.

The Procedure We Used to Make our Choices

We have reviewed more than 1,700 books and articles that we collected during several Center research projects on diversity. One of these projects, research on female executives, produced the book *Breaking the Glass Ceiling: Can Women Reach the Top of America's Largest Corporations?* (Updated Edition) by the lead author (with White and Van Velsor; Addison-Wesley, 1992). The majority of the works, however, were collected in the course of research for the Guidelines on Leadership Diversity (GOLD) project which the lead author has documented in *The New Leaders*.

To help the reader evaluate our choices, we'll summarize our selection procedure. First, we did an initial screening of the 1,700 articles and books collected for research for *The New Leaders* and for previous research projects, and we refined our choices overall and for each step (while at the same time adding additional works). After drafting descriptions of most of the works we planned to include, we brought in other professionals via a two-step review process.

Seven experts from inside and outside the Center for Creative Leadership responded to our list of references (according to the five steps) and added or deleted works based on their judgment. These experts, named in the Acknowledgements section, had expertise in research, consulting, or training, and their input shaped our decisions. They helped us identify a few works to delete, but mostly suggested additional books and articles that we subsequently reviewed and, in some cases, added to the digest. Next, some of these same reviewers agreed to critique our descriptions of certain works. They reviewed about forty percent of the descriptions, which helped guide us in our analysis and emphasis of the work.

We used five criteria to select the work included in this digest:

• The work is current, as indicated by a publication date of 1988 or later. (In a few cases we included work published earlier in the 1980s, which we felt was necessary to present a unique perspective, approach, or database that is still relevant.)

• The work is practical, or application-oriented, as opposed to purely theoretical or clearly aimed at an academic audience.

• The work presents unique or important information in a clear, well-written form.

• The work is easily accessible, through a bookstore, library, publishing company, or other firm. Articles available only by contacting the author were ruled out, although a few are noted in the Appendix.

• The work helps round out information about one of the five steps or for the digest as a whole.

We made changes in our list and descriptions after each step of the review process. No additions to the list were considered after July 1992.

What You Won't Find in This Digest

There are a number of books and articles that do not address diversity but which contain information important to a diversity effort. These are beyond the scope of this book, but we

encourage anyone serious about making an intervention to
become familiar with additional resources. These bodies of
literature include:

• **Organizational change.** The five-step process for
developing diversity that we recommend here and originally in
The New Leaders is essentially a map for organizational
change. The principles of effective change efforts and the
learning-from-change attempts represent valuable input into a
diversity initiative. (An excellent resource in this area is the
1983 book, *Assessing Organizational Change: A Guide to Methods, Measures, and Practices,* edited by Stanley Seashore,
Edward Lawler, Philip Mirvis, and Cortlandt Cammann [John
Wiley & Sons].)

• **Management/executive development and career
development.** Since development of talented individuals is a
key goal in many diversity efforts, this literature can be very
helpful when effective principles and practices can be appropri-
ately generalized to nontraditional managers. Because much of
the research and practice in this area is based solely on white-
male employees, practitioners should be cautious about adopting some recommendations.

• **Strategic human resource management.** The connection is obvious between this area and a diversity effort
aimed at developing a range of human resources. This body of
literature links the human resource to business goals and
emphasizes the long-term nature of this management challenge.

• **Psychology and sociology.** Individual and collective
factors affect an organization's ability to change. This literature can shed light on such issues as how to change prejudicial
attitudes, how to help newcomers adjust and cope in ways that
increase retention, and how to keep groups from splitting into
"insiders" and "outsiders."

Also there are quite a few very good written works about
women (skills, decisions, and characteristics that make them
successful as managers, etc.), which could not be included

because of their publication date or simply because there has been so much written about women that we had to be especially choosy.

We also reluctantly eliminated several recent papers that fit all of our criteria except that of being easily accessible. There is excellent material being presented at conferences, for example, that is not yet published and is available only on request from the author. A short list of some of these references is included in the Appendix. Our cutoff date for adding references was July 1992, so there may be additional works presented at conferences in August and later that would be helpful. Readers may want to contact organizations like the Academy of Management and the American Psychological Association (both hold an annual convention in August) to obtain the program of presentations and perhaps follow up with authors.

Many insightful theoretical works were also excluded because they did not meet our criterion of being application-oriented. This work is often useful background for a diversity effort, but it may require patience and concentration for managers to appreciate these contributions. We favored practice-oriented works in which the implications for diversity activities were more explicit.

We ruled out a number of recent articles that have appeared in the popular press only because these appear on a regular basis, outdating the current ones quickly. These pieces are often useful because they are credible, easy to read, and they include current statistics and short company profiles and examples. We encourage practitioners to keep abreast of the latest newspaper and magazine articles such as those we have included and to use them whenever possible.

Case studies are included throughout the digest, such as in the "Awareness Training" subsection under Step 3. We believe that the most helpful case-study information is built into literature that explains or compares them, but we also encourage readers to use case studies to shed light on topics about which little has been written, such as the role of top management in a diversity effort, and the characteristics of effective accountability tools. Since only one article appears in the "Accountability" subsection under Step 3, the case studies and General References section are especially important to supplement this limited information.

Step 1...

DISCOVER (AND REDISCOVER)
DIVERSITY PROBLEMS
IN YOUR ORGANIZATION

The barriers to advancement affect many nontraditional managers across many organizations, but the ways in which those barriers operate can vary dramatically from one organization to another, and even among divisions or regions of the same organization. Finding and understanding the most significant problems in your organization (or in your part of the organization) is a basic first step in making headway on diversity issues.

One benefit of uncovering problems on your own is that they have special meaning within your company or institution. When managers and employees are directly involved in the investigation and have clarified the issues for themselves, they are more likely to invest in solutions. Also, problems change over time, so it is important to periodically assess which problems still exist and which are most critical at the moment.

This category includes references that describe the kinds of problems often experienced by nontraditional employees in organizations, problems relating to the "glass ceiling" and other barriers that are so prevalent that they deserve consideration in most investigations. The section is quite lengthy because a number of references document the problems faced by people of color and white women in organizations. These articles and books, however, also provide information about assessment tools, with an emphasis on ways to determine how employees perceive their environment.

Assessment

Steinberg, Ronnie J., Lois Haignere, and Cynthia H. Chertos.
    "Managerial Promotions in the Public Sector: The Impact
    of Eligibility Requirements on Women and Minorities."
    Work and Occupations. 17 August 1990, pp. 284-301.

Step 1

This study identifies the point in a multistage-promotion
process at which women and people of color are blocked from
advancement. The authors studied public agencies in New York
State since promotional processes are more structured and
regulated in the public sector than in corporations, making it
easier to identify institutional barriers. Two sets of data covering 1,381 promotions at salary grade levels 23 to 38 were
analyzed. It was found that promotions occurred because of
administrative transfers or were based on a competitive examination which included five stages: eligibility, application,
qualifying, passing the exam, and being selected.

The key finding in this research is that eligibility requirements represent the primary institutional barrier to the promotion of women and people of color. Eligibility requires being
employed in a job title explicitly listed in an exam announcement. The authors note that, "On average, only 12% of the pool
of eligibles were women and only 4% were minorities." (The
data are based on promotions received in the late 1970s, but
the authors present evidence that the same conditions exist
today.)

These results refute the assertion from previous research
that the examination is the primary barrier, and they qualify
the finding that the "rule of three" (excluding all candidates
except the top three scorers on the exam) blocks qualified
women and people of color by being too rigid. The researchers
determined that women (minorities) constituted 12.5% (5.8%)
of those who applied to take an examination, 12.1% (5%) of
those who qualified, 13% (4.2%) of those who passed, and 16.1%
(4.6%) of those selected for promotion, indicating that the
examination itself did not constitute a systematic institutional
barrier to their promotion.

The researchers also examined the "rule of three" and
found that if the selection lists were changed to be based on the

top five or the top ten, the lists that women would have placed on would have increased by 15% and 25% respectively, and the lists that people of color would have placed on would have increased by 2% and 8% respectively. Ensuring that more women and people of color were considered, however, would not guarantee their selection. In fact, the probability of their being selected decreases as the list is expanded from the top three to the top ten.

The authors recommend eliminating job-title eligibility requirements, because job titles are often based on occupational segregation that has undervalued positions traditionally held by people of color and white women and no longer effectively serve as "decision-making shortcuts." This research indicates that job titles and other eligibility criteria for promotion should be examined for bias or obsolescence in many organizations, and that new career ladders may need to be designed. Organizational audits might include these factors and their impact on promotional decisions.

❖❖❖

Thomas, Roosevelt R., Jr. *Beyond Race and Gender: Unleashing the Power of Your Total Work Force by Managing Diversity.* New York: AMACOM, 1991. 189 pages.

This book illustrates through three case studies how organizations might approach and carry out a change process for developing diversity. The instruments, data, and action-planning techniques shown in these examples (particularly the cultural audit tools) are valuable aids for practitioners undertaking a diversity effort. They also help put into operational terms Thomas's concepts about cultural "roots" and appropriate strategies for "managing diversity," which are outlined in his 1990 article in the *Harvard Business Review* (see Step 2, page 45).

Through a composite case history, Thomas tracks the efforts of one organization, Compound Products, Inc., in order to conduct a cultural audit and take action based on the results. A detailed interview guide gives specific questions to ask in this process. Thomas then points out how the recommended actions would differ if management chose an affirmative-action approach to solving diversity problems, a valuing-differences approach, or his preferred approach of managing diversity by modifying the core culture so that it works for everyone. Action steps for the latter approach are outlined in a five-year plan, complete with outcomes.

Step 1

The most elaborate case study depicts the change effort of Avon Products, Inc., beginning with the research stage in which two sets of interviews were conducted. The interview guide for senior and human resource managers and the guide for other managers within the company are presented, which can be used or adapted by other practitioners. This case study reports two important ways that Avon responded to the audit data. First, a task force on managing diversity was created to define diversity, identify its benefits for the company, and analyze work-force issues. The task-force recommendations included educational programs and improvements in the staff-development process. Second, a new human resource strategy was created, along with a five-year plan for its implementation. The plans included getting the right people in the right place, reinforcing and rewarding performance, and helping people learn and grow. Action steps and milestones are laid out, year by year, as another good example of how a change process works.

Another case study of a Fortune 500 company is presented, which includes a thirteen-question interview guide, detailed responses by demographic group, and the management response to the data. Thomas also covers issues of an organization's readiness for change and the link between diversity and total-quality management. Questions frequently asked about diversity and the change process are also addressed in the final chapter.

This book, with its detailed examples of tools and techniques, is a useful resource for practitioners to frame issues and to develop their own instruments and plans. Thomas's emphasis on asking the right questions and acting on the responses is also likely to help practitioners get a diversity effort off to a good start and keep it on track.

❖❖❖

U.S. Department of Labor. "Corporate Management Reviews" (Chapter 5), In *Federal Contract Compliance Manual.* Washington, D.C.: U.S. Department of Labor, November 1991. 83 pages.

Chapter 5 of the *Federal Contract Compliance Manual* is an outcome of the Department of Labor's Glass Ceiling Initiative. It was recently added to the manual (originally issued in 1979) by the Office of Federal Contract Compliance Programs. The chapter describes the corporate management reviews now being conducted by the OFCCP to determine whether federal contractors "ensure equal employment opportunity in developing, selecting and treating mid-level and senior corporate managers." The background and questions in this chapter provide a map for organizations to evaluate their own practices in terms of their impact on management-level traditional and nontraditional employees.

Step 1

As a tool for self-evaluation, the most useful parts of this chapter are sections 5G through 5K (pages 18-54). These sections cover general-management practices as well as practices that may exclude nontraditional managers or candidates for management. Brief explanations and a series of questions are included in sections dealing with general qualification standards, external hires (including executive search firms and employee referrals), internal development (including succession planning, promotion and transfers, movement across units and within headquarters, performance appraisals, visibility, training, mentoring and networking), retention (including total compensation, bonuses, stock awards and options, and recognition awards and honors), and terminations.

In the section on external hires, for example, there is an explanation of how executive search firms are typically used, followed by questions such as, "Have minorities and women, as well as others, been hired from among search firm referrals? Have they been among those referred? If not, was any effort made to expand the candidate pool?" Questions about the succession-planning process include: "How does that process work? Who identifies? Based on what factors? Does a person need to be sponsored? Down to what level of the work force does it extend? Are there any written materials describing the process and offering guidance on selecting and developing participants?"

This is a useful and practical guide to a self-analysis of practices geared not only toward developing diversity but also toward productive human resource management in general. This chapter may be particularly relevant for government contractors who may face an OFCCP audit, and to any organization prioritizing its management practices in preparation for a diversity effort.

Step 1

Barriers

Bell, Ella Louise. "The Bicultural Life Experience of Career-oriented Black Women." *Journal of Organizational Behavior* 11:6, November 1990, pp. 459-477.

This article reports on part of a study of the bicultural life experiences of black professional women—how these women deal with both the black and the white cultures in which they participate. It deals with the problem of confronting the hurdles created by the push and pull between the two cultures and how these barriers can be overcome in black women's career and personal development.

The theoretical background of the research is based on Bell's concepts of biculturality and Levinson's life structure of social contexts. Black women who choose a bicultural life structure may hold on to their African-American roots without being totally assimilated into the dominant white culture in which they work. Movement from one context to the other, however, can cause identity conflict, tension, and other problems.

This study involved self-assessment workshops in which small groups of women provided data about their personal networks, experiences, major life roles, and stressful events. The research team also used in-depth, five-hour interviews with a few women to get detailed biographical portraits. Their responses show high levels of satisfaction with their careers, and indications that they use divergent thinking, creativity, risk-taking, and boundary spanning as adaptive responses to their biculturality. On the negative side, however, they experience tokenism in organizations that are not adaptable or accommodating, and they regularly struggle with the contradictory demands of the different cultures. One problem they confront is that they often have inadequate knowledge of the requirements of their career roles but they feel pressured to perform exceptionally well to compensate for both their race and sex.

Step 1

This article addresses the career problems of professional black women, a group that tends to be ignored in the literature. The work, however, is exploratory, and so the implications of these findings are tentative at best. Its significance is in recognizing the extra demands that many women of color face and the need to factor these demands into career-management systems intended to develop diversity.

❖❖❖

Bonilla-Santiago, Gloria. *Breaking Ground and Barriers: Hispanic Women Developing Effective Leadership.* San Diego: Marin Publishing Co., 1993. In Press.

Bonilla-Santiago investigates "how Hispanic women's educational and employment backgrounds, career goals, aspirations, cultural differences, obstacles, and styles of leadership have contributed to, or made a difference in, the way they have managed their lives as they developed into leaders." She interviewed fifty female Hispanic leaders and asked them how they overcame barriers and became successful. Using open-ended questions, she allowed them to talk as long as they wanted and about whatever they felt was important. Their actual names are used (by their choice) in the book.

More than half of the book is devoted to the biographies of seventeen of the fifty Hispanic women leaders. The biographies are told in their own words and reveal their feelings and personalities. These seventeen Latinas in the public and private sectors are: Polly Baca, the first Hispanic woman to serve in any state senate in the U.S.; Marta Benavides, Salvadoran Minister and first woman to be ordained as a Baptist pastor in her country; Maria Antoinetta Berriozobal, former Councilwoman, city of San Antonio, Texas; Blandina Cardenas, Associate Director of the Office for Minority Concerns, American Council of Education, Washington, D.C.; Sylvia Castillo, Director of Marketing and Business Development at Seabury Hall Academy in Hawaii; Miriam Colon, the Artistic Director and Founder of the Puerto Rican Traveling Theater in New York City; Dr. Alicia Cuaron, Vice-President of Source One, Inc.; Patricia Diaz-Dennis, Federal Communications Commissioner from 1986-1989; Fern Espino, Dean of Student Development, GMI Engineering and Management Institute, Flint, Michigan; Nely Galan, Manager of WNJU-TV, New York City; Lena Guerrero, first Hispanic woman appointed Commissioner of Railroads and Transportation in Texas and the second Hispanic woman to be elected to the Texas House of Representatives; Dolores Huerta, First Vice-President and co-founder of the United Farm Workers of America; Gloria Molina, first Hispanic woman elected to the Los Angeles County Board of Supervisors; Esther Novak, Director of Urban Affairs, AT&T; Guadalupe C. Quintanilla, Assistant Vice-President for Academic Affairs at the University of Houston, Texas; Helen Rodriguez-Trias, M.D., Department of Health, pioneer in combining the fields of pediatric medicine and grass-roots politics in New York City; and Ileana Ros-Lehtinen, first Hispanic woman elected to the U.S. Congress.

Bonilla-Santiago sought answers to three primary questions from these women: Which leadership characteristics do most successful Hispanic women leaders possess, and how are these different from those of men and of women in general? What are the impediments to Hispanic women in becoming leaders? How can emerging female Hispanic leaders be identified, and what programs could provide support and information to them?

This researcher discovered that one of the primary barriers to Hispanic women's career development occurs at a very young age. Due to their socialization combined with the lack of emphasis on young Hispanic girls' needs to get a good education, and economic hardship, many Hispanic girls' talent and potential is hidden for years or, worse, for a lifetime. Both sexism and racism were perceived as major barriers to advancement. Differences in derailment factors for Latina and white women are also examined.

The author criticizes the (white) feminist movement for failing women of color, because it does not recognize their unique needs and perspectives. For example, a major difference between white feminist leaders and Latina feminist leaders is that the former can choose to ignore the political and social context around them as they concentrate on their careers, but many Latina women (and likely other women of color) devote much of their professional lives using this context in their daily work.

Step 1

The voices of Latina leaders often go unheard in the literature about diversity, so this book makes a unique contribution. It helps give managers a better understanding of the differences and similarities within this group of successful women as well as those between this group and other groups of leaders.

❖❖❖

Cabezas, Amado, Tse Ming Tam, Brenda M. Lowe, Anna Wong, and Kathy Turner. "Empirical Study of Barriers to Upward Mobility of Asian Americans in the San Francisco Bay Area." In *Frontiers of Asian American Studies.* Gail Nomura, Russell Endo, Russell Leong, and Steven Sumida, eds. Pullman, WA: Washington State University Press, 1989, pp. 85-97.

This study attempts to uncover barriers to Asian-Americans' advancement. The authors analyze how several factors relate to mobility barriers and reasons for job changes— Asian ethnicity, gender, age, educational-attainment level, and duration of employment. They surveyed 308 Asian-American (mostly Chinese-American) managers, professionals, and technical workers, and grouped their responses into five factors: company-related barriers (corporate culture, management insensitivity, the lack of informal networking, mentors, and role models), discrimination, family-related geographical residence constraints, situational factors (such as shrinking advancement opportunities), and a lack of oral or written communication skills.

The researchers found both employee-related barriers and structural or societal barriers. Language difficulty was cited as a significant problem, but company-based barriers were found to be the most serious impediment. They claim that the substantial investment made by many Asian-Americans in education and work experience yield low returns to advancement, and this is a problem that employers are better equipped than individuals to address. Race discrimination also emerged as a significant barrier. The women surveyed cited sex discrimination and work-family conflicts as more serious barriers than the men did. The more educated Asian-Americans frequently cited racism and a lack of mentors as significant barriers, perhaps because they have greater knowledge of racism or are more likely to consider it a societal problem rather than a personal one.

Step 1

The authors claim that the relatively high number of job changes made by those in the study was associated with a lack of role models and a lack of informal networks. The respondents who predicted that they would not be with the same company in five years (26%) cited management insensitivity, communication problems, and a lack of role models. The authors point out that "this finding is important for employers who . . . want to reduce the cost of high employee turnover." Reasons given by men and women for leaving the company were similar, and about 75% cited career advancement as their primary reason.

No statistically significant differences among the different Asian-American groups were found, but most of these groups were very small. The authors do point out peculiarities and sensitive areas which can help managers recognize not only the differences between Asian-Americans and other Americans but also those among the Asian-American groups themselves.

This work is useful in designing assessment tools and other diversity activities because it is one of only a few that specifically addresses issues important to Asian-American employees. It also helps sensitize managers to more subtle differences within a broad ethnic group that could be overlooked in an investigation or in designing diversity activities.

❖❖❖

Catalyst. *Women in Corporate Management: Results of a
Catalyst Survey.* New York: Catalyst, 1990. 44 pages.

This report describes the results of a survey undertaken
to determine: the status of women in management at major
U.S. corporations, whether women truly are in the "pipeline"
for senior-management positions, and perceptions of the qualities women need to advance and the barriers they face. Survey
respondents included Fortune 500 and Service 500 CEOs (241) $\quad$ *Step 1*
and human resource professionals (224). A second Catalyst
report using this database, "Women in Corporate Management:
Model Programs for Development and Mobility," is described in
Step 3, page 57.

Women represent less than 5% of senior managers in
most of the companies surveyed; financial service companies
(insurance in particular) reported higher figures than manufac-
turing or other corporations. CEOs' responses indicate they
want to advance women, mainly because they see an "increased
presence of talented women" (78%) and "need to use the most
talented human resources" (62%). Most CEOs reported that
women in management already have the competencies and
traits needed to compete with men for top-level posts, but
women remain clustered in staff functions that have limited
advancement potential. Most CEOs (79%) recognized barriers
to women's advancement: stereotyping/preconceptions (81%),
management's aversion to taking risks with women in line
positions (49%), and a lack of careful career planning and
planned job assignments (47%), among others.

Survey responses concerning work and family programs
and flexible work arrangements indicate that the latter are not
available to professional and managerial employees in 40% of
the responding companies, and that they are least available to
employees in jobs most likely to lead to top management—
production-and-facilities line positions and supervisory jobs.

The report concluded that "the strategies that companies
have in place to address the advancement of women are not
designed to address the specific development needs of women"
which include assuming line positions and a broad range of
functional experience. Women comprise 25% or less of "high-
potential employees" in about 60% of the companies surveyed,
and most companies report no programs to target women for

the developmental experiences needed to qualify them for top posts. The report goes on to say that the strategies reported for advancing women are not only too general, but they are also a low priority, perhaps because cost containment (the highest priority reported) has not been associated with retention of experienced, high-potential female employees.

Step 1

Survey data can be difficult to interpret. The phone interviews conducted as part of this study do help, although the dependence on human resource professionals for interview data is a concern. Overall, this research is useful for identifying women's barriers to advancement and pointing out issues that should be explored in developing an internal investigation. It also alerts managers to the potential gap between problems and practices. Solutions need to be deliberately matched to the problems identified in an internal investigation.

❖❖❖

Cox, Taylor, Jr., and Stella M. Nkomo. "Differential Performance Appraisal Criteria: A Field Study of Black and White Managers." *Group & Organization Studies.* Vol. 11, March-June 1986, pp. 101-119.

The research presented in this article relates to advancement barriers for blacks. This study indicates that different criteria based on race are used to evaluate the job performance of managers. The authors discovered that black managers' social behavior, an indication of how well they "fit in" with established norms, is an important factor in their overall performance evaluation. Social behavior, however, does not appear to be important in evaluating white managers' performance. The authors hypothesize that the more complex set of performance criteria used for black managers represents "a subtle form of covert discrimination," and they speculate that these extra criteria may be used at lower levels to keep "task-capable" blacks from advancing into management.

The research on race and sex bias in performance evaluation is inconclusive, but the authors note that prior studies have paid little attention to subtle forms of discrimination—if the overall ratings did not differ by race, the conclusion was that discrimination did not exist. In contrast, this study examined the evaluation criteria, and it involved managers in an actual organization (rather than a laboratory setting) who rated their own subordinates. Twenty-two middle managers, mostly white, were asked to rate their black and white subordinates using a performance-appraisal form. The respondents believed that the appraisal form was being tested for possible use within the organization. Items on the form related to general-performance traits, task performance, and social behavior.

 Step 1

The results of this study are consistent with other researchers' findings that many black managers perceive they are subjected to different or extra performance expectations. Solutions to this problem offered by Cox and Nkomo include: providing rater training, including greater emphasis on understanding cultural and ethnic differences; instituting more objective appraisal processes such as behaviorally anchored rating scales (BARS) or management by objectives (MBO); supplying more than one evaluator for each subordinate, such as a committee of superiors or peer-evaluation techniques; and increasing the proportion of people of color in the work force. One limit of this study is that only blacks and whites are compared, so the effect on other nontraditional managers can only be inferred.

❖❖❖

Dickens, Floyd, Jr., and Jacqueline B. Dickens. *The Black Manager: Making It in the Corporate World.* New York: AMACOM, 1991. 446 pages.

This revised version of the 1982 book examines the unique developmental needs and problems facing black managers, proposes a step-by-step process to overcome barriers, and offers suggestions to organizations and individual managers to effectively use the diverse work force.

The authors' developmental model illustrates four phases in blacks' career development: entry, adjustment, planned growth, and success. They describe the attitudes, emotions, behaviors, and job skills important in each phase for the survival and success of black managers. In the job mastery phase, for example, in which black managers who have broken the "glass ceiling" are placed, rewards for a job well done are often internal and are based on the black managers setting and reaching their own high standards.

The authors also suggest internal, external, and environmental strategies for maximizing the chances for success in an organization. Internal strategies include, for example, black executives controlling their own psyches by managing their rage and creating an effective personal style. An external strategy is managing key relationships with others in the organization. Environmental strategies consist of dealing with the specific corporate culture through strategic management, the effective use of power, and black development. Other recommendations are also offered such as recognizing the importance of networking and developing a positive self-image.

The final section of the book describes an approach to managing diversity. Four basic building blocks for managing a diverse work force are: obtaining new knowledge about diverse groups, developing employees, recruiting diverse employees, and supporting and developing (to retain) employees. Part of the first step is to access the added value that different groups bring to apply to a task, including assets such as their experiences, values, behaviors, skills, and talents. Recognizing generalizations—not stereotypes—about groups is an important part of this step.

The authors offer thirty-seven suggestions for making diversity work in an organization, which range from taking responsibility for your own attitudes, behavior, and job performance to learning about others' cultures and using differences to enhance productivity and service. They give examples of techniques for recruitment, mentoring, information sharing, providing support, training and development, education, and enforcement being used by organizations to more effectively utilize the diverse work force. This book can be used both by organizational leaders who are developing a diversity initiative and by individual managers of color for their own development.

❖❖❖

Feminist Majority Foundation. "Empowering Women in Business." Washington, D.C.: *Feminist Majority Foundation,*
1991. 20 pages.

This report presents data and information about the
representation of women in the work force, in management, in
the executive ranks, and on corporate boards. For example, one
fact presented is that only 2.6% of top-executive officers at
Fortune 500 companies are women. It breaks the data down by
industry and by company so that readers can assess how their
industry and company compare. For example, in the aerospace
industry, women make up 3.6% of the directors and 2.5% of the
officers.

Step 1

The report describes the barriers that women face. It also
describes female executives' thoughts on the causes of the
"glass ceiling," which include: job segregation, the old-boy
network, sex discrimination, sexual harassment, and lax enforcement of antidiscrimination laws. These researchers also
reviewed polls and published statistics to determine how many
women are feminists in the U.S. today. They discovered that
despite the media's claim, feminists are the majority. An historical account of the feminist movement is provided.

This report refutes ten myths about women in business,
such as "It is just a matter of time" until women reach parity
with men. According to their data, it will take 475 years—until
the year 2466—before women reach equality with men in the
executive suite. The myth that "The younger generation of men
is more supportive" is also countered. Research has shown that
younger men are actually retaining "consistently negative
attitudes toward women as managers." Also refuted is the
myth that "Any woman can make it to the top if she's compe-
tent and works hard. That's how men make it, after all." This
report claims that corporations are not the meritocracy that
we've all been led to believe. For example, "More than half of
the board chairmen of the Fortune 500 companies are the sons
of former chairmen."

Five strategies for change are outlined. These are: explode
the myths, push for gender balance, organize with other feminists, consider legal alternatives, and use the media. Thirty
resources (with addresses and phone numbers) for speakers

and for obtaining current research are provided at the end of the report.

This paper provides very useful data for presentations, training sessions, and for triggering responses for group discussion. It helps direct practitioners to the continuing problem spots and to the considerable progress which still needs to be made in organizations. Although the five strategies for change may be more relevant to social activists, they are also useful as management techniques in organizations.

Step 1

Fernandez, John P. *Survival in the Corporate Fishbowl: Making It into Upper and Middle Management.* Lexington, MA: Lexington Books, 1987. 314 pages.

This book provides information about the career problems employees are likely to encounter and strategies they might use to overcome them. Diversity issues, such as race and sex differences, are addressed as one set of problems many employees confront. Three other types of problems common to all employees are bureaucratic social structures (based in part on Weber's theory of bureaucracies [*The Theory of Social and Economic Organization,* Oxford University Press, 1947]); human neurosis; and the American value system as related through the socialization process. Fernandez' database is large—survey responses from 12,000 managerial and nonmanagerial employees of various ethnicities and both sexes at 13 companies—and his recommendations are based on an even larger cumulative research base as well as his personal experience.

The author makes recommendations about career problems common to all employees as well as problems specific to people of color, women, and white-male employees. He explains how advancement works, using theories of advancement as a backdrop for data about employees' beliefs about what it takes to get ahead. He notes the demand for homogeneity in promotion decisions, referring to "managerial cloning" as a process that "reinforces the notion that those who are at the top deserve to be there." His advice to all employees about how to play the corporate game emphasizes getting to know people who can influence your career, understanding that they themselves are trying to advance and gain power, and he also stresses that they understand themselves. He advises employees to be conscious of issues related to manipulation and other uses of power, issues in building your team, and your attitude toward work.

Chapters dealing with the additional problems of being a woman or a person of color in a corporation highlight the continuing existence and subtleties of prejudice and provide insight into corporate culture. They cover issues such as exclusion from informal work groups, dual-performance standards, and stereotypes. He also discusses the problems of sexual harassment and work and family conflict that many women experience, and he indicates that additional issues for people of color include problems with oral and written skills, difficulty in organizing, and dealing with paranoia. A chapter on white-male employees' problems addresses the belief that white men are now disadvantaged because of affirmative-action programs. Fernandez describes seven "realities" to counter this perception (which are also included in his book, *Managing a Diverse Work Force*; see General References section, page 115): Corporate America is unfair to all; image is vital to success; competition is keen; white men are still advantaged; the concept of reverse discrimination is based on lies; nothing excuses poor performance; and white men must adjust to diversity.

Step 1

This book clearly emphasizes individual employees' problems and career-advancement tactics. Only six pages are devoted to "what corporations must do," so Fernandez' advice to human resource professionals is very limited. The book does contain research-based information and tools useful in designing an investigation. This information can also be used to create other diversity interventions as part of a corporate initiative.

❖❖❖

Greenhaus, Jeffrey H., and Saroj Parasuraman. "Job Performance Attributions and Career Advancement Prospects: An Examination of Gender and Race Effects." Forthcoming in *Organizational Behavior and Human Decision Processes*.

This study, part of a larger research project by these authors and Wayne Wormley, examined bias in job-performance evaluation. The authors hypothesized that the job success of female and black managers would be attributed by their supervisors to different causes than the success of men and whites, and that these supervisors' performance attributions would change as they had more experience with the managers. They also hypothesized that supervisors' assessment of managers' career-advancement prospects played a role in their performance attributions.

Step 1

The researchers collected survey data from 748 black and white managers and professionals, and their supervisors, working in three companies. Their findings clarify some barriers that hinder the progress of nontraditional managers. They found that female and male managers rated as moderately successful were equally likely to have their performance attributed to ability, but that was not true in the highly successful group where women's performance was less likely to be attributed to ability. Black-managers' performance was consistently more likely to be attributed to help from others than to ability and effort, in comparison to white-managers' performance. The authors claim that these findings suggest that some supervisors discount the successful performance of black managers— and some female managers—through their reluctance to attribute it to high ability.

Over time, the relationship that develops between a supervisor and a black manager tends to reduce race differences in performance attributions. The researchers, however, cite the need for more objective performance measures since many black managers appear to be "at risk" in newly developed relationships with supervisors—their job success is more likely to be attributed to ease of the job and luck rather than ability. Also, supervisors saw less favorable career prospects for black managers than for whites.

The authors did not find a "double whammy" effect for black female managers in that they did not have the most unfavorable attributions. They did find that, overall, race differences in job success and performance attributions were stronger than sex differences. The authors caution against treating sex and race differences as if they had the same impact in areas of career development such as these.

This study helps explain the subtlety of bias and its impact on career advancement. Even when the level of performance is rated the same for a traditional and a non-traditional manager, the attribution process may limit the nontraditional manager's career prospects. This subtlety needs to be incorporated into internal investigations and considered in the design of remedies for differential treatment. This study makes an important contribution because it involved actual managers and their supervisors, in contrast to much of the work on performance-evaluation bias which is done with college students as subjects.

Step 1

❖❖❖

Knouse, Stephen B., Paul Rosenfeld, and Amy L. Culbertson, eds. *Hispanics in the Workplace.* Newbury Park, CA: Sage Publications, 1992. 292 pages.

Many of the articles in this book claim that a dearth of research exists regarding the situation for Hispanics in corporations and businesses in the United States. The authors have undertaken a sizable effort to pull together and analyze the information that does exist and to undertake new studies themselves.

Part I, "Employment Factors," contains statistics which can help educate people about the conditions for Hispanics in the workplace. Part II, "Problems at Work," examines the characteristics of litigated employment discrimination cases involving Hispanics and the occupational and economic stressors among Hispanics. Part III, "Mentoring Support Systems for Work," explores the mentoring process for Hispanics and unique considerations which organizations should take into account when developing a mentoring program in which Hispanic managers will participate. Part IV, "Hispanic Women and Work," reports on the experiences and barriers that characterize the careers of Hispanic women. Different authors investigate both Chicana (women of Mexican descent in the United States) and Puerto Rican women. Part V, "The Hispanic Experience in Government and Private Work Sectors," covers issues specific to Hispanics in the military, Hispanics in the federal government, and Hispanic managers employed in Anglo businesses.

In Part VI, "Hispanics in Anglo Business," Ferdman and Cortes report on some of the cultural themes which came up in their study, including differences in leadership styles due to a different orientation toward people, a direct approach to conflict, and a flexible attitude toward hierarchy. These and other findings in this book offer promising ideas for assessing barriers and for designing diversity practices that accommodate Hispanics as well as other nontraditional managers. This is a useful resource for anyone interested in the status of Hispanics in management and in the overall work force.

Step 1

Lefkowitz, Joel, and Linda Iorizzo. "Gender Differences in Job Attitudes and Personalogical Variables." *ERIC Document Reproduction Services,* No. ED 291 986. September 1987. 33 pages.

These researchers examined previous studies of sex differences in job attitudes, values, preferences, and other reactions to work, and hypothesized that many of the reported differences may be due less to the sex of the individual and more to their occupational or pay level. They examined this hypothesis first in the literature and second in their own study.

They found that Hulin and Smith (1964) provoke this investigation by demonstrating that it is not a person's sex that causes differences in job satisfaction, but rather the entire constellation of other variables which tend to vary with sex, such as pay, job level, promotion opportunities, and societal norms that causes what appears to be sex differences in job satisfaction. After reviewing studies which have examined sex differences, the authors note that studies which report sex differences tended to be ones which did not control for the variables mentioned by Hulin and Smith.

Lefkowitz and Iorizzo studied a sample of 365 men and 357 women from nine organizations and a professional association. They investigated sex differences on 23 job reactions and 26 dispositional variables. Examples of job reaction variables include satisfaction from work and security needs. Examples of dispositional variables include supervisory ability and importance placed on advancement. Initial analyses revealed 19

significant differences reflecting traditional sex-role stereotypes. Almost all of these differences "disappeared," however,
when analyses were used to control for differences between
men and women in job characteristics, age/tenure, levels of
education, income, and occupational group. Income and occupational level together accounted for every observed significant
sex difference in job reactions. In other words, as the researchers point out, "when one controls statistically for the fact that
the men tend to have higher-level, higher-paying jobs than the
women, there are virtually no differences between them in the
many job attitudes assessed in this study."

 Step 1

This work is particularly relevant during the first steps of
assessing the problems within your organization since it
counters a common assumption that women are less motivated,
involved in, and satisfied with their jobs, and that they use less
initiative, maturity, authority, and power; all of which are
proved by this study to be false assumptions. Understanding
that many so-called sex differences are tied to other factors
such as pay and rank is an important step in designing an
internal investigation.

❖❖❖

Morrison, Ann M., Randall P. White, Ellen Van Velsor, and the
    Center for Creative Leadership. *Breaking the Glass
    Ceiling: Can Women Reach the Top of America's Largest
    Corporations? (Updated Edition).* Reading, MA: Addison-
    Wesley, 1992. 231 pages.

In this updated edition, two current contextual factors
and some recent research have been added to the largely
unchanged body of the 1987 book. The book addresses several
questions: What does it take for women to enter the executive
suite? What factors propel women up, what derails women, and
are these factors the same for men? Do women need the same
opportunities for development as men?

Extensive interviews with seventy-six women and other
senior executives at or near the general-management level in
their corporations shed light on the problems that continue to
confront high-potential women in management and on the
kinds of development needed to help women overcome these

problems. Most of the book is devoted to describing how these women broke through the glass ceiling into the executive ranks and to advising other women who want to do the same.

Step 1

The researchers discovered that these female executives experienced three levels of pressure: the job itself, their pioneer role in their job, and their family obligations. The six success factors identified by senior executives as most important are: help from above, a track record of achievements, the drive to succeed, the ability to manage subordinates, willingness to take career risks, and the ability to be tough, decisive, and demanding. The three most serious derailment factors are: the inability to adapt, wanting too much for oneself or for other women, and performance problems. A comparison with the factors important for male executives revealed several specific differences and, in general, that women are expected to have more strengths and fewer faults than their male counterparts.

Two types of lessons that these executive women learned was that it is not enough to work hard, and it is not enough to work smart. This research indicates that women must use what are often contradictory skills, such as learn the ropes, take control of their career, build their confidence, rely on others, go for the bottom line, and integrate life and work. Three extra elements that contribute to women's success are credibility, advocacy, and luck. Some of the limits felt by the women interviewed are a perception of "no road to the top," a feeling of being "hemmed in," a vanishing support system, and exhaustion.

This new version assesses the impact of two recent developments: the federal government legislation and monitoring of women's workplace issues through the "Glass Ceiling Initiative" and the 1991 Civil Rights Bill; and the newly recognized business imperative of including women and other traditionally underrepresented groups in the management ranks. These developments along with results from recent research studies by the authors and others are factored into the implications and recommended action for women and their employers. This research is useful in making managers more aware of the myths and barriers many women face in corporations, and in designing assessment tools that include a variety of dimensions relevant to women (and probably other nontraditional managers).

❖❖❖

Petrocelli, William, and Barbara Kate Repa. *Sexual Harassment on the Job: What It Is and How to Stop It.* Berkeley, CA: Nolo Press, 1992. 242 pages.

Step 1

The two attorneys who wrote this reference guide provide information on both informal and formal ways of confronting sexual harassment. It is intended for both the individual who is harassed and the organization that wants to prevent it. The authors describe the evolution of sexual-harassment laws, provide a state-by-state overview of the laws, dispel myths about sexual harassment (such as, sexual harassment is inevitable when men and women work together), and provide numerous real and hypothetical examples of sexual harassment. Quotes are given from diverse sources and provide perspective to the topic. Sample letters, forms, and policies are provided.

The authors define sexual harassment as "any unwelcome sexual advance or conduct on the job that creates an intimidating, hostile, or offensive working environment." Different manifestations of sexual harassment are described, ranging from sexual innuendos and misogynist humor to rape. They point out that this behavior is usually motivated by fear, power, or hate, and that it is often aimed at getting a woman to leave her job or the company. "Sexual harassment often accomplishes informally what laws against sex discrimination theoretically prohibit: gender-based requirements for a job." If a woman is sexually harassed and subjected to pressure, degradation, and hostility that her male co-workers don't have to endure, then it becomes that much harder for her to compete for the job and for advancement. "Sexual harassment on the job is almost always an abuse of power designed to discourage women from continuing in the work force or getting more desirable, better paying jobs."

The four legal issues which are examined in sexual-harassment suits and which a plaintiff must be ready to argue are that the conduct was: (1) sexual in nature, (2) unreasonable, (3) severe and pervasive, and (4) unwelcome. Each of these is described in detail and examples from real and hypothetical cases are provided for clarification. A suggested process to follow if harassment continues after an employee confronts a harasser is to collect evidence, keep a detailed journal, talk with friends, talk with co-workers, organize a group, and get copies of work records. At this point the employee should have enough information to pursue a formal action.

Step 1

The authors describe elements of a good sexual-harassment policy. For example, prohibited behaviors must be explicitly stated and guidelines for reporting sexual harassment should be offered. A thorough workplace investigation process should include interviewing the complaining employee, witnesses, and the alleged harasser, and evaluating evidence, followed by prompt action. A sample sexual-harassment survey is offered. Special complaint processes for U.S. government employees and union members are also described.

Legal remedies under the U.S. Civil Rights Act and the EEOC (Equal Employment Opportunity Commission) generally include: reinstatement and promotion, back pay and benefits, money damages up to $50,000-$300,000 depending on the number of people employed in the organization, injunctive relief (court order to change its policies), and attorney's fees. State laws often cover sexual harassment as well (a state-by-state review of the laws is provided). Common law torts are sometimes used to compensate a harassed employee for her personal injuries. When, how, and why to pursue the different legal avenues are described in several chapters.

Many organizations are addressing sexual harassment as an important topic. There is a lot of mystery, however, around what constitutes sexual harassment, how it should be handled internally, and what legal rights victims may exercise. This book is a useful resource for sifting through the mass of questions, concerns, and issues that arise in dealing with sexual harassment.

Powell, Gary N. "One More Time: Do Female and Male Managers Differ?" *Academy of Management Executive* 4:3, August 1990, pp. 68-75.

Powell addresses the question, "Do male and female managers differ in their basic responses to work situations and their overall effectiveness?" He reviews evidence from a num-

ber of studies that spans three viewpoints: no differences between women and men in management (despite possible differences in the general population); differences according to
masculine/feminine stereotypes and socialization; and differences opposite to sex-role stereotypes, because female managers
have countered social norms.

Powell reviews studies on sex differences in behavior,
motivation, commitment, and subordinates' responses. He
shows that in most cases there were no real differences. Sex
differences were absent in task-oriented behavior, people-
oriented behavior, effectiveness ratings of actual managers, and
subordinates' responses to their managers. He points out that
confusion arises in this research arena because some laboratory
studies have indicated differences, but when these studies are
done in organizations as field studies, the differences disappear.

Step 1

The author concludes that since no real differences exist in
needs, values, and leadership styles between female and male
managers, then organizations should "minimize the creation of
sex differences in managers' experiences on the job." He suggests that organizations should be gender-blind in hiring and
promoting managers, except when consciously trying to offset
the effects of past discrimination, that they avoid segregated
training-and-development programs, that they make mentors
more available to everyone, and that they not automatically
assign women to staff positions assuming that "women have a
monopoly on human resource skills." This data helps managers
understand that presumed differences between female and
male managers may limit their career progress far more than
any actual differences, and also how this problem should be
dealt with in designing diversity activities.

The lack of sex-related differences is important to recognize during the early stages of program design. The results
imply that organizations should be conscious not to relegate
women to staff positions because of stereotypes, they should not
provide special training (like assertiveness training) for women
which plays on these stereotypes, and they should think seri-
ously about any implications of programs they implement (such
as mommy and daddy tracks which may limit the manager's
career even upon returning to the organization).

❖❖❖

Rosener, Judy B. "Ways Women Lead." *Harvard Business Review,* November-December 1990, pp. 119-125.

Step 1

Rosener cites data from a survey showing that female and male managers who make the same amount of money describe their leadership style differently. Though Rosener recognizes that not all women are interactive leaders, and that some men may use this leadership style, she suggests that interactive leadership is a more natural style for women than for men. She also argues that organizations could benefit from recognizing and accepting different leadership styles.

Rosener sent a questionnaire to members of the International Women's Forum and to the men nominated by them who were to be in similar organizations with similar responsibilities. She found that women often report they exhibit a leadership style which she calls "interactive" leadership, which elsewhere has been termed "transformational" leadership. It involves "getting subordinates to transform their own self-interest into the interest of the group through concern for a broader goal." This style is contrasted with "transactional" leadership which views job performance as a series of transactions with subordinates (rewarding services rendered and punishing inadequate performance).

Interactive leaders encourage their staff's participation from aspects of work as varied as setting performance goals and determining strategies. Not only do they listen to others' input, but they also share their power and their information. They use two-way communication channels. Interactive leaders enhance the self-worth of others by valuing their opinions, by empowering them and giving them information, and using their enthusiasm for their work to energize their staff. Rosener argues that this nontraditional leadership style can be effective in organizations.

Perhaps as informative as the article itself are the thirteen responses to Rosener's argument in the following issue of the *Harvard Business Review* under the heading "Ways Men and Women Lead" (January-February 1991, pages 150-160). Several academics and businesspeople who responded to the article agreed with the overall results of her study, and some disputed her findings, which reported that both the female and the male managers (who were paid equally) paid their female employees an average of $12,000 less than their male employees.

This article and the responses to it show the spectrum of opinions about whether sex differences exist in leadership style. These opinions affect how problems are perceived and the kinds of solutions that get adopted in organizations. Managers can use this information to shape an organizational analysis and to help decide which diversity practices may be warranted.

Step 1

❖❖❖

Russell Reynolds Associates, Inc. *Men, Women, and Leadership in the American Corporation.* New York: Russell Reynolds Associates, Inc., November 1990. 55 pages.

This research analyzes manager-style executives and leader-style executives to see if there are significant differences between female and male executives. The results show that "women in both staff and line positions were more likely to be leader-style executives than their male counterparts." This study refutes the belief that women are not effective leaders and raises questions about how to better recognize female leaders.

The participants in this study consisted of 164 men and women in upper management of Fortune 500 companies. These managers were mostly white, between 40 and 49 years of age, and had salaries of over $200,000. The participants were surveyed about three concepts: (1) leadership orientation, (2) executive-success factors, and (3) corporate environment. The survey questions are included in the report.

A comparison of the characteristics of leaders versus managers is in the introduction. The report notes that leaders are risk-takers, they find problems, and they are innovative and concerned with vision; managers are risk-averse, like to fix problems, are concerned with tasks/people, and want to stabilize and create order. The findings show that more female executives, in both line and staff positions, displayed leadership orientation than their male counterparts. Also, women in staff positions displayed a leadership orientation more often than men in line positions.

This research argues against traditional stereotypes about female executives, and it raises questions about whether companies are taking advantage of the qualities of female managers.

❖❖❖

Step 1

Tashjian, Victoria W. *Don't Blame the Baby: Why Women Leave Corporations.* Wilmington, DE: Wick and Company, 1990. 10 pages.

This research argues against the assumption that women leave corporations to raise children. The author's main point—don't blame the baby—supports other recent research that the turnover of women is higher than that of men because of women's dissatisfaction with their company (opportunities for growth, development, and advancement) and not because of work-family conflicts. Although day care and family benefits are important, the author notes, they will not prevent women from moving to another employer. This report highlights the need to investigate problems before investing in inappropriate solutions.

The conclusions are based on interviews with 58 men and 52 women from northeastern Fortune 500 companies, comparing respondents who stayed five or more years with their company with those who left after five years. The results show 73% of the women left to join another company compared with only 7% who ended up staying home, and that most women (like many men) left for career growth and development (55%), to move up the corporate ladder (36%), or to start a business (27%). This research also shows that men (26%) were more likely than women (9%) to say that children played a role in their decision to quit a job.

The author also discusses why so few women reported that they were "highly likely" to remain with their company (35% vs. 77% of the men). Comments of the women interviewed revealed that "because of the high personal price they pay for having a career, professional women will not settle for dead-end jobs." Contradictory research exists on whether the turn-over rate for female managers is higher or lower than for male managers. The 1990 Catalyst study (see Step 1, page 17), for example, reports lower turnover for women.

Only a few general recommendations are given for how corporations can better retain women: Learn the key issues for women, establish a plan, act on and communicate the plan, and demand results. This report's main value is that it alerts managers to dysfunctional assumptions about career barriers women face, and it illustrates how an investigation of problems can help avoid wasting time and money.

Step 1

❖❖❖

U.S. Department of Labor. *A Report on the Glass Ceiling Initiative.* Washington, D.C.: U.S. Department of Labor. 1991. 25 pages.

This report documents the Department of Labor's effort to determine if barriers to advancement exist for women and people of color and how these barriers can be eliminated. The report is based on research done from 1989 to 1991 involving compliance reviews of nine randomly selected corporations; discussions with representatives from business, labor, women's, and civil-rights organizations; and evaluations of independent research. It concludes that indeed a glass ceiling exists at a much lower level than first thought.

The Glass Ceiling Initiative consists of four parts: (1) internal education within the Department of Labor, (2) a pilot study investigating nine companies, (3) public awareness of diversity and encouragement of voluntary efforts, and (4) recognition and public awards to those companies actively working on removing barriers to advancement. Although the Department of Labor concedes that the nine organizations used in their study are not necessarily representative of all organizations, they do identify several general findings which applied to all nine companies. They recommend that these findings be considered by all organizations attempting diversity initiatives. For example, there was a general lack of adequate records for evaluating initiatives. There was also a lack of monitoring appraisal and total-compensation systems that determine salary, bonuses, incentives and perquisites for employees. Common barriers to the advancement of women and people of color were the reliance on recruitment by networking, the lack of opportunities for people of color and women to take advanced-education programs and career-enhancing assignments, and the lack of accountability for equal-opportunity responsibilities at senior-executive levels.

This study pinpoints key problem areas to investigate and incorporate into a widespread change effort. It gives more credibility to the existence of an often invisible glass ceiling, and provides useful suggestions concerning what needs to be addressed to penetrate it.

Step 1

Webb, Susan L. *Step Forward: Sexual Harassment in the Workplace. What You Need to Know!* New York: Mastermedia, 1991. 116 pages.

The author argues that six key elements need to be present in order for sexual harassment to be effectively prevented: Top-management support is required, a written policy statement must be posted, procedures for getting and handling complaints must be communicated and effective, complaints must be handled, all employees should be trained, and follow-through must be done. A sample policy statement illustrates the important ingredients in an effective policy: statement of purpose, legal and behavioral definitions of sexual harassment, importance of the problem, suggestions for how employees should handle harassment and how organizations should handle complaints, disciplinary action, and names and phone numbers of individuals to call.

Webb offers training tips based on her own experiences. Getting management to support training, ensuring that a policy against sexual harassment is posted prior to the training, and covering grievance procedures are some of the pointers offered that are often overlooked. Being prepared for frequently asked questions, no matter how basic, is also important, and a chapter is dedicated to reviewing these questions and suggesting answers to them. To support her emphasis on the importance of training, Webb cites the 1988 WORKING WOMAN Sexual Harassment Survey (WORKING WOMAN, 342 Madison Avenue, New York, NY 10173) showing that it is "34 times [as] expensive [as training] to ignore the problem" of sexual harassment (based on a comparison of absenteeism, turnover, and lost productivity costs to training costs).

Webb reviews steps that managers, supervisors and individual employees can take to stop and prevent sexual harassment. Managers can publicly notify all employees of the company's sexual-harassment policy and educate them about what the policy means. They can ensure that all employees and new hires participate in sexual-harassment training. And managers must deal with sexual-harassment claims promptly. Supervisors can facilitate action and communication around sexual-harassment claims and observed sexually harassing behavior (even if unreported). Individual employees must first admit when sexual harassment has occurred and then develop a strategic plan for dealing with the problem that balances considerations of stopping the behavior, keeping their job, and ensuring their continued effectiveness and productivity on their job.

Step 1

Finally, short- and medium-length case studies and questions are given which can be worked through individually or in groups to provide stimulation for discussion and awareness. Also statistics on the frequency of sexual-harassment complaints and costs associated with ones taken to court are provided.

This book emphasizes companies (rather than individuals) more than another book in this section—*Sexual Harassment on the Job* (Petrocelli and Repa; page 29). Another difference between the two books is that *Sexual Harassment* is in bullet form, punctuated by quotes and commentary, and reads somewhat like a workbook. *Step Forward* approaches the topic more from the employer's standpoint. Many of the same cases are used in each book, but in *Step Forward* they seem to be primarily related to their impact on employers.

This book would be useful to trainers, managers, and individuals. The case studies and training tips provide both framework and substance for sexual-harassment training. The review of the law and examples of sexual harassment is useful information for the manager and supervisor.

Step 2...

STRENGTHEN TOP-MANAGEMENT COMMITMENT

The commitment of an organization's leaders to diversity is so important it warrants emphasis as a separate step in the process of developing diversity. This does not mean that commitment occurs only at this point in the process; rather, the spirit and actions that characterize commitment are needed at every step. To engage in self-analysis, as in Step 1, without any semblance of commitment from top management would indeed be foolhardy, since identification of the problems without any follow-up to solve them would probably exaggerate the problems. The internal investigation is put as the first step, however, because it is likely to help convince executives that problems do exist and to help clarify the nature of those problems. Reports of problems in other organizations may be dismissed as not relevant, but an inside investigation provides more compelling evidence for top management.

Commitment from the top of an organization may be the most important factor contributing to the success of a diversity effort. The role of top management includes defining the fundamental approach to be taken with regard to diversity and providing resources needed to implement meaningful solutions.

This category includes some information about how to gain top-management commitment in an organization, but most of these references cover either the rationale for diversity in senior executives' own words or the background needed for many senior executives and others to decide on an appropriate approach to developing diversity.

Lapid-Bogda, Ginger. "How to Win Senior Management's
    Support for Diversity." *AMA,* March 1992, p. 7.

In this article, Lapid-Bogda explains how diversity-
change efforts that require the attention of individuals and
groups from diverse backgrounds, human resource professionals, and senior management can be effected. She states that
conventionally, affirmative action was relegated to human
resources. But for diversity efforts to be truly successful, senior
management must communicate, chart, and mandate a specific
vision regarding the importance and necessity of diversity
programs and policies.

Step 2   The author contends that senior management is rarely
inattentive to diversity by design. More often top management
is unaware of the importance of diversity efforts, due to their
own (frequently privileged) backgrounds and the high demands
on their time, energy, and focus. The author suggests several
guidelines to follow when trying to obtain top-management
commitment.

First, she suggests interviewing top management about
their opinions on diversity. This assessment is helpful in recognizing differences among the senior-management team and in
identifying allies. Next, directly link diversity to the bottom
line with specifics. Third, provide top management with data
about complaints, potential lawsuits, and hiring and retention
problems. This will interest them, help them perceive the
relevance of the efforts, and should increase their support.
Fourth, discover "what they lose sleep over." For example, if
one of their main concerns is market share, try to find a way to
expand the product or service into diverse markets. Next,
provide diversity training for senior management. Finally, link
diversity to other organizational initiatives such as total-
quality management, self-managing work teams, or career
development.

This is the only reference we were able to find that focuses on outlining ways to win senior management's commitment and support for diversity efforts. It has many recommendations which are practical and attainable and which can be
found few other places. The author has written other (unpub-
lished) papers (see Appendix) which go into slightly more
depth.

CEO Advocates of Diversity

Alster, Judith, Theresa Brothers, and Holly Gallo, eds. 75th Anniversary Symposia Series. *In Diversity is Strength: Capitalizing on the New Work Force.* Report Number 994. New York: The Conference Board, Inc., 1992. 21 pages.

This report gives the reader some insight into several top managers' views on diversity issues. Top executives from American Airlines, Inc., Allstate Insurance Co., U.S. West, Inc., and Control Data Corp. provide us with their opinions on current forces for change and methods of managing these forces. Charles Handy's "The Age of Unreason" provides an analysis of business developments and how they benefit or inhibit diversity. In "Whither the Work Force" by Delores Wolfe, former VP, Personnel Resources at American Airlines, an account is provided of how the work force—and business—is changing and alerts the reader to the need for businesses to take some responsibility for educating, developing, and training workers. In "Managing Diversity: A Full-Time, Top-down Commitment," Wayne E. Hedien, Chairman and CEO of Allstate, recognizes that managing diversity is a process and not a program. He describes his company's Diversity Action Teams and their learnings.

Step 2

Richard D. McCormick, President and CEO of U.S. West, counters a common myth in "Making Sure Diversity Works at U.S. West." He disagrees with the statement that if people are hired without regard to race, sex, or national origin, the cream will rise to the top. He argues that "work-force discrimination is alive and well and insidious" and that in order for change to occur top management must exert a concerted and continuous effort to counter barriers to the advancement of women and people of color—through actions, not words.

In "Turning Diversity Into Opportunity" the business imperative of diversity is described from the point of view of a once-manufacturing-company-in-danger to a service-company-with-opportunity. Lawrence Perlman, President and CEO of Control Data describes how changes within the basic structure of the company have been complemented by—and, in some ways, catalyzed by—changes in the work force. He cautions that it isn't easy to turn diversity into an opportunity. "It brings a certain degree of chaos to an organization. It creates tension, disagreement and discontent, but without differences of opinion and perspective . . . you risk having an environment where everybody thinks alike, acts alike, and comes to the same conclusions. That's what got us into trouble in the first place."

A question-and-answer section provides executives' answers to questions such as, "Is managing diversity just old wine in a new bottle?" and "Do you have any evidence that your diversity efforts have made your company more competitive?" The last piece, "Will Diversity Win?" by Charles Handy, provides tips and wisdom through stories and examples of ways in which managing diversity can be implemented.

Step 2

These articles are very brief and to the point—ideal for busy top executives to read to determine what other top executives think—and do—about diversity. This could be used as pre-work for diversity training offered to top management.

Estrada, Alfredo J. "CEO Roundtable on Workforce Diversity." *Hispanic,* January-February 1992, pp. 28-34.

Hispanic magazine brought together several CEOs of major corporations to discuss the value of work-force diversity. Participants included M. Anthony Burns of Ryder Systems, Inc., Peter R. Kann of Dow Jones & Company, Inc., Robert C. Winters of The Prudential Insurance Co. of America, and Paul A. Allaire of Xerox Corporation. Estrada reports the reasons given by these executives for investing in diversity and a few examples of the types of diversity activities being used in these companies.

At Ryder, for example, work-force diversity is incorporated into business objectives, with hiring goals tied to managers' bonuses. CEO Burns comments that, "What we've done is given economic incentives to make the right decision on diversity." Ryder also gives scholarships to Hispanic MBA students and supports an Hispanic Council of employees. Burns notes that the council helped change Ryder's advertising program to better address the Hispanic market. At Dow Jones, CEO Kann points out, recruitment is an important activity, not only on campuses but also through support of professional organizations such as the National Association of Hispanic Journalists.

These companies are all considered to be well-managed and represent a cross-section of corporate America. The rationale behind these CEOs' support for diversity and the brief examples of activities used for recruitment, development, and accountability may help other executives understand how business is affected by diversity.

❖❖❖

Lee, William S., and Reuben Mark. "Family, Minority Motivation Requires Highest CEO Priority." *Financier.* Vol. 14, April 1990, pp. 27-31.

Step 2

Based on a panel discussion at a conference on work and family policies, this article highlights the views of two chief executives committed to antidiscrimination and better accommodation of nontraditional employees. William S. Lee, Chairman of Duke Power, and Reuben Mark, Chairman of Colgate-Palmolive Co., declared that corporate programs that accommodate family needs and advance antidiscrimination policies rank among the highest responsibilities for CEOs in motivating their work force. They claim that work/family and anti-discrimination policies increase productivity and retention of employees and agree on the need for policies to increase accountability among management. Mark, for example, includes these policies in an eight-year plan to revitalize the company.

Regarding the bottom-line cost savings of family policies, Mark said, "The first semester of any psychology course is going to tell you about the effect of a person's problems on their productivity. By definition, if we can reduce external pressures, improve the way the people think about themselves, their family life, and the company, productivity is going to increase." The importance of setting goals, measuring progress, and publicly posting both (or rewarding their attainment) was discussed.

Although there is limited description of the actual policies of the companies, basic guidelines are outlined: Be flexible, walk your talk, set goals and timelines, and hold managers accountable for results. The importance of commitment from the top cannot be stressed enough, and these two chairmen make it obvious that progress is more difficult without it. Lee's decision to lay off only white-male workers sixteen years ago rather than sacrifice the progress made toward nondiscrimination is an example of the courage required of committed top executives.

Step 2

This article's value is in the presentation of arguments that support the contention that productivity is increased by policies that are sensitive to family and discrimination concerns. Though it shouldn't be necessary to prove that diversity practices will increase productivity, it is much easier to convince executives to invest resources if they feel it will positively affect the bottom line. Their disagreement on some points, such as the role of government in promoting equal opportunity, is useful for promoting discussion on the issues.

Stages/Paradigms for Organizational Development

Palmer, Judith. "Three Paradigms for Diversity Change Leaders." *OD Practitioner.* Vol. 21, March 1989, pp. 15-18.

Palmer describes three paradigms—the "Golden Rule," "Right the Wrongs," and "Value All Differences"—for approaching diversity initiatives in organizations. She notes that the different beliefs and expectations of each often create confusion among change leaders in a diversity effort, so making these clear from the start is important for success. Palmer outlines for each paradigm how diversity would be defined, the vision and approach to change, and what the priorities would be.

The Golden Rule paradigm (do unto others as you would have them do unto you) recognizes only individual differences and not prejudice or systemic oppression. Since everyone is special and different, this paradigm holds, everyone should be appreciated and treated the same. According to the author, the weaknesses of this approach are that the golden rule is applied from one's own frame of reference, without regard for the traditions and preferences of others, and that sex or race differences are considered to be no more impactful than individual differences.

The Right the Wrongs paradigm addresses the historical injustices that have disadvantaged people of color and women. These groups are targeted, often one by one as they reach a critical mass in an organization, to be hired, advanced, and rewarded more equitably. This approach to diversity is closest to the affirmative-action concept, but with more attention to understanding and capitalizing on the unique characteristics of each group to improve the organization's performance. It is similar to Taylor Cox's (1991; see Step 3, page 58) model of a multicultural organization. The author contends that because group differences and histories can create a "we versus they" tension, this approach may fuel backlash and infighting.

The Value All Differences paradigm recognizes differences associated with the heritage, characteristics, and values of many sex, ethnic, and other different groups, as well as the uniqueness of each individual. This approach, like Cox's multicultural organization model, assumes that organizations must change to accommodate a wide range of workers. Palmer notes, however, that this paradigm is so new that there are no proven methods or even a common language associated with it.

These paradigms form the basis for different, potentially conflicting approaches to developing diversity. Understanding and communicating fundamental models and belief systems like these may be a critical element of any diversity effort.

❖❖❖

Thomas, Roosevelt R., Jr. "From Affirmative Action to
    Affirming Diversity." *Harvard Business Review,* March-
    April 1990, pp. 107-117.

Thomas, who directs the American Institute for Managing Diversity, affirms the reasons for managing diversity and supplies ten guidelines by which an organization can accomplish it. He begins by describing how organizational climate has changed since affirmative action was first implemented thirty years ago. He explains why the five basic premises of affirmative action are now obsolete and how the traditional approach to diversity has resulted in a self-destructive cycle of crisis, action, relaxation, and disappointment. In the current scenario of assimilated diversity, he argues, affirmative action must be supplemented by "managing diversity," or the challenge of "get[ting] from a diverse work force the same productivity we once got from a homogeneous work force."

Thomas's ten guidelines outline a step-by-step process of organizational change. The guidelines are: Clarify motives and goals for managing diversity; expand your focus beyond race and sex to include heterogeneity in its broadest form; conduct research via a cultural audit; make changes in the assumptions (such as appropriate roles for family members), systems (such as promotion, mentoring, and sponsorship), and models (such as "doer" managers) used in organizations; help your people pioneer; apply the special consideration test; and continue affirmative action. Thomas advocates contributing to everyone's success, rather than trying to produce an advantage for only blacks or whites, or only women or men.

Step 2

This article is likely to prompt thinking and discussion about diversity issues. Semantics, however, may pose a problem for some. If, for example, affirmative action is confined to entry-level hiring practices (as Thomas uses the term) then, by definition, affirmative action cannot promote upward mobility and alternatives are needed. Also, if a weakness of affirmative action is that it conflicts with "the meritocracy we favor" in organizations, then how do we factor in the contradictory premise that the cream doesn't naturally rise to the top of the organizational hierarchy but rather is "pulled or pushed to the top by an informal system of mentoring and sponsorship"? These and other issues are likely to be debated, which may be a very constructive exercise as part of a training program or a meeting of an executive committee or a task force, for example, to increase awareness and understanding of diversity problems and potential solutions.

Historical and Legal Background

Bearak, Barry, and David Lauter. "Affirmative Action: The
   Paradox of Equality." Three-part series. *Los Angeles
   Times,* November 3-5, 1991, Section A. 10 pages.

This three-part series provides an historical view of
affirmative-action efforts and the 1991 Civil Rights Act (CRA
'91). The reporters' goal is to help us understand "the legalistic
stutter steps" that brought about the new civil rights bill,
which explicitly states what Congress avoided saying for
twenty-seven years: that "It is proper to use racial preferences
to remedy the wrongs of the past."

Step 2

The first part in the series, entitled "Tense Steps to
Ending Racial Bias," describes the climate of the 1960s that led
to the passage of the 1964 Civil Rights Act. The landmark legal
case, Griggs v. Duke Power, is described from the perspective of
the suit's originator, Willie Boyd, and it is traced from before
the case's inception to the final verdict written by Chief Justice
Warren E. Burger: "If job requirements act as 'built-in head
winds' against a minority group, the employer had better be
able to show that those standards are essential to the work;
there must be a 'business necessity' for the requirement to be
legal." The burden of proof that the company's policies are not
discriminatory is clearly placed on the employer. The contrary
principles of the 1964 Civil Rights Act's Title VII—"color blind-
ness" and "racial bookkeeping"—are also described in the first
part. These two goals have since produced much of the contro-
versy around the 1964 legislation, including the association of
quotas with "racial bookkeeping" that has provoked charges of
reverse discrimination.

The second part of the series, entitled "U.S. Anti-Bias
Regulations Disrupt Lives, Workplaces," describes the landmark legal case of reverse discrimination filed by Brian Weber,
a white man. This case was heard by the Supreme Court in
1979 and focused on "legislative intent" with regard to the 1964
Civil Rights Act. The court ruled against the plaintiff, arguing
that due to "the nation's long and vexing history of inequality,"
Congress must have intended the bill to open opportunities; if
this had to be done through race-conscious hiring, then this

was not discrimination. Finally, after fifteen years of ambiguity, the 1964 Civil Rights Act was better defined and had the endorsement of the high court.

Part three in the series, "1991 Rights Bill a Return to Earlier Path of Bias Redress," opens with a description of how President Reagan's administration slowed affirmative action and ends with a description of the events that led up to President Bush signing the 1991 Civil Rights Bill. In January 1989, the Supreme Court heard the case of Wards Cove Packing Co. v. Antonio, and it made its first statement contrary to the Griggs decision. Their opinion stated that employers were no longer burdened with proving the business necessity of hiring requirements. The burden was shifted to the employee to prove that the company's job requirements were irrelevant to its business performance. A new civil rights law was drafted—one by the Democrats and one by President Bush—both calling for a return to the Griggs decision. The Democrats' bill passed and was promptly vetoed by Bush as "a quota bill." Finally, Bush agreed to a compromise bill which strikingly resembled the ones he had previously opposed.

Step 2

This documentary is useful in making managers more aware of the events and circumstances behind the legislation we have today. It provides the historical and legal background from which diversity practitioners work. Knowledge of where we've come from gives us perspective on where we need to go. This article is one piece of that background.

Edsall, Thomas Byrne, and Mary D. Edsall. "When the Official Subject is Presidential Politics, Taxes, Welfare, Crime, Rights, or Values . . . the Real Subject is RACE." *The Atlantic Monthly,* May 1991, pp. 53-86.

This article provides a contextual framework for viewing race and racism in this country. The authors claim that "race has played a critical role in the creation of a political system that has tolerated, if not supported, the growth of the disparity between rich and poor over the past fifteen years" and they bring in various points and data to support that claim.

They examine two tracks on which race (black/white) relations are moving. On the one track, there has been remarkable integration: an increase in the black middle class, a reduction in some racial stereotypes that fuel prejudice, and an increase in managerial and professional jobs held by blacks. On the second track, however, the poorer blacks' situation is worsening: There has been an increase in crime, welfare dependency, illegitimacy, drug abuse, and a generation of young people unwilling to stay in school or take menial jobs.

The authors argue that the marked increase in the income of the affluent and the marked decrease for the middle class and the poor has contributed to a stronger racial split between whites and blacks. Presidential elections have served to worsen this split. Working-class whites are now frequently made to feel threatened by poorer blacks, they note, as the Republican Party has worked to polarize whites and blacks. The authors use detailed examples of presidential elections, voting patterns, changes in ideologies, suburbanization, and the influence of crime and values on whites' and blacks' opinions of themselves, and others, to provide proof of the increasing antagonism experienced between these groups. All of these influences are then shown to be compounded by current economic and demographic forces. Whites' and blacks' struggle over the shortage of jobs, resources, and benefits is becoming increasingly bitter and irreconcilable.

Step 2

This article is recommended reading for anyone who wonders, "Why are people of color so angry?" It examines the social context for understanding the impact of race in organizations. One possible limitation is that while ethnic groups other than blacks and whites are occasionally mentioned, they are largely missing in this analysis of racial dynamics. It is likely, however, that many managers will find this article contributes to a broader perspective on the issues of diversity.

"Race in the Workplace: Is Affirmative Action Working?" *Business Week,* July 8, 1991, pp. 50-63.

The first two pages of this article pictorially represent the progression toward integrating people of color in the workplace.

It begins in 1941 with President Roosevelt's orders to defense contractors to cease discriminatory practices in hiring, proceeds to the backlash against integrating non-whites in the 1980s and 1990s, and ends with Bush's veto of the 1990 Civil Rights Act. The article depicts the contradictory opinions surrounding affirmative action: One side argues that affirmative action hasn't done enough, and the other side counters that white males are now the victims of discrimination.

Step 2

The complexity involved in affirmative action and diversity efforts is illustrated through stories within the main article and several sidebars. We are made aware of the wide range of responses to affirmative action. Some companies lose interest in black advancement once a hiring goal has been met. Other companies go far beyond the requirements and actively recruit, develop, and promote people of color because they recognize both the moral and the economic imperative of doing so. The author maintains that even among blacks there are differing opinions about affirmative action. For example, Shelby Steele, a professor, argues that affirmative action works against their race by stigmatizing blacks in organizations as unworthy and inferior. Others are dissatisfied with affirmative action because it doesn't require organizations to do anything to retain or promote their black work force, only to hire them.

Some companies that want to actively recruit, develop, retain, and promote a diverse work force, but who want to avoid the emotionally-loaded term *affirmative action,* have embraced the term *managing diversity.* These organizations do more than just hire the right number of people of color. They also find ways of acclimating the hires to the organization's culture, ensure that their voice is included in hiring, promotion, and development decisions, provide developmental opportunities, and offer professional feedback.

Sidebars are used to demonstrate the use of professional advocacy groups by Avon Products, Inc., as a barometer on how the company is doing in their diversity efforts; illustrate the complex factors that determine whether a company has met or has failed to meet their affirmative-action goals (and how a lack of attention to this can hurt the company); describe Hughes Aircraft Company's efforts to retain and advance people of color during a period of dramatic downsizing; describe Monsanto's diversified efforts to advance and retain women and people of color using exit interviews to determine why they were leaving and establishing a "Consulting Pairs" program to train employees to serve as consultants on race and gender issues; and discuss the problem of so many groups (women, Hispanics, Asian-Americans, and blacks) demanding a piece of a shrinking pie.

This article provides a clear overview of the complex history of affirmative action. In general, it provides the reader with a sense of how far we've come, how far we need to go, what we've learned in the past, and how organizations are using these learnings to develop more innovative and effective programs and policies within their organizations.

Step 2

Zall, Milton. "What to Expect from the Civil Rights Act." *Personnel Journal,* March 1992, pp. 46-50.

A quick overview of how the 1991 Civil Rights Act (CRA '91) will affect employers is presented in this article. Zall addresses critics' concern that this new act will increase discrimination litigation since the burden of proof has been returned to employers' shoulders, and damage awards are potentially more lucrative. He counters that employers can prevent this by being well-informed of changes in employment laws and by preparing themselves. The civil rights act changes the way courts will rule on certain actions, practices, and behaviors. This article serves to clearly and quickly inform the reader of recent changes that management should be aware of.

This act reverses seven Supreme Court decisions. One change involves giving the employer the final burden of proof of a "business necessity" for an employment practice that has a discriminatory impact (for example, the requirement of the ability to lift a certain weight has a discriminatory impact on women). This contradicts the prior requirement (after Wards Cove Packing Co. v. Antonio) to prove a "business justification." Also, it is wise for employers to once again validate any employment tests or criterion to see if they have a positive correlation with specific job requirements. Employers may have relaxed this practice after the ruling on the Wards Cove Packing Co. case. (For more information on this case, see "Affirmative Action: The Paradox of Equality" in this section, page 47.)

Reversals of other decisions have had the following impact: Employees are now protected from post-hiring discrimination as well as discrimination in hiring practices; employers are not permitted to avoid liability in mixed-motive discrimination cases by proving the company would have taken the same action regardless of the proven discriminatory motive; challenges to seniority systems are permitted when employees become subject to them; protection is extended against discrimination to U.S. citizens employed abroad by U.S. owned companies; the use of race norming (adjusting scores and test results on the basis of race, sex, etc.) is prohibited; and (in favor of employers) reverse discrimination suits which challenge consent decrees when "actual notice" is given to all affected parties is now disallowed.

Step 2

This information is provided both in detail within the article, and in a quick reference sidebar. Other suggestions to employers are offered in another sidebar, such as the advice to monitor your language and actions to prevent making statements indicating racist or sexist stereotypes, and to try to detect the discriminatory effects of employment practices. Civil rights legislation is increasingly complex, and the new law changes how civil rights cases are treated. This article may help managers avoid costly lawsuits since it provides enough detail to understand the changes, while also providing a brief outline of the changes so that managers can quickly assess what these changes are.

Step 3...

CHOOSE SOLUTIONS THAT
FIT A BALANCED STRATEGY

A vast array of diversity activities exists. It is very difficult to choose some practices over others when virtually all of them have merit. Finding an effective mix of solutions is a tricky exercise, and matching solutions to the most pressing current problems is full of complexity. Combatting prejudice, for example, covers hundreds of techniques that are interactive and sometimes elusive. Also, many managers have run into trouble by adopting popular practices rather than matching practices to the problems identified in their particular organizations. Solutions need to be tailored and adapted to an organization's priorities, history, and culture.

An extensive array of options may be needed, because no single practice is likely to have a significant, lasting impact on diversity. Yet the dilemma is clear: Although concentrating on only one or two practices will have only a limited or temporary effect, spreading resources too thinly over a number of practices will doom them all. How can you choose a reasonable set of solutions? *The New Leaders* (Morrison; Jossey-Bass, 1992) provides some guidelines that can take some of the frustration out of this process.

Step 3

The references in this section provide information about and examples of the three types of diversity practices: recruitment, development, and accountability. There are more references in this step than in the others because much attention has been focused on development activities such as awareness training and mentoring. To the extent that these practices are called for in an organization, the information in these sections will help design them in effective ways. Unfortunately, references to accountability tools are sorely lacking. We found only one article that fit into the "Accountability" section, so readers must look for guidance in the general references or elsewhere.

"Benchmarking HR: Measuring Up to the Leaders." *Human Resource Executive,* June 1992, pp. 23-37.

This article identifies and profiles "best practices" in seven human resource areas: training and development, pay for performance, health-care benefits, work and family, diversity, recruitment, and relocation. All of these practices, not simply the ones in the diversity category, help managers understand the range of options available and also help them visualize an effective mix of practices.

Human Resource Executive, in collaboration with a consulting firm, conducted a review of existing human resource policies. Readers were asked to nominate best HR practices, and a database of more than 575 human resource best practices was searched. The criteria were that the practice support the business's overall needs, that it be innovative, that it apply quality management principles, and that it enhance the employee-company relationship. The research team screened all of the nominations and selections and sent the finalists to a panel of human resource executives who selected five best practices in each of the seven categories. These are described in the article.

Step 3

Companies recognized as winners for their work-force diversity initiatives are Gannett Co., Inc., TRW, Avon Products, Inc., U.S. West, Inc., and Apple Computer, Inc. Gannett's practices include institutionalizing diversity by linking it to managers' bonuses and using a high-level Equal Employment Opportunity Advisory Committee to review progress. A software-based tool at TRW, based on a thirty-minute questionnaire completed by employees, is used to address networking patterns according to sex and ethnic groups and any differential promotion rates. Apple's multi-cultural diversity effort includes interaction between employee groups and senior management as well as relationships with twenty-one "minority, women's, and disability-oriented professional organizations."

Examples of innovative work-family policies include the provision of $1,500 for adoption assistance at Fel-Pro Inc., child-care subsidies based on income level at Stride Rite Corp., and a three-year unpaid leave program at IBM for new and adoptive parents (with full benefits) and for employees who have elderly parents or relatives requiring care. IBM also offers a preretirement program which allows employees to try retirement or test a new career with the guarantee of being able to return to the old job.

In the training and development programs selected, a common thread emerged: They are continuous and ongoing. Several of the companies (Federal Express Corp., Motorola, Inc., USAA, British Columbia Telephone Company, and Walt Disney Co.) offered yearly training and development for all levels of employees. Perhaps the most innovative program, run by Walt Disney, identifies local high-school students who are on the verge of dropping out and provides them with schooling, training, and job experience. Upon receiving their diplomas, students are encouraged to apply for full-time permanent employment with the company.

These and other human resource practices have saved some companies millions of dollars and contributed to their workers' productivity, according to this article. Other researchers have suggested that companies which are successful at managing their employees' needs in general tend to be the same companies that are successful at managing a diverse work force. The examples in this article may help managers see more possibilities for action.

Step 3

❖❖❖

Blanchard, Fletcher A., and Faye J. Crosby. *Affirmative Action in Perspective.* New York: Springer-Verlag, 1989. 211 pages.

The policy of affirmative action is critically analyzed in this book—its importance, advantages, limitations, problems, and complexities. The introduction asks the reader to assess hiring and promotion standards. The authors point out that just as a blind student may be given a standing ovation at his graduation from business school while his sighted colleagues are not, so too should we be impressed more by the good performance of a female, despite sexism, or a person of color, despite racism, than by the equally good performance of a white male. They recommend specific and justified criteria: Is the winner the one who crosses the finish line first or the one who clocks the fastest time? Unless one slants the finish line to compensate for the shorter distance of the inner track, the different criteria may yield different winners.

The first section of the book reviews the history of federal legislation, executive orders, and federal court cases regarding the application of affirmative-action policies. Case studies describing problems with the hiring standards of New York City firefighters and the ineffective affirmative-action policies of the federal government are used as examples. The next section examines varying reactions to affirmative-action policies, such as the mixed reactions of targeted groups who benefit from affirmative-action policies yet resist policies which appear inequitable, and the backlash from those who perceive themselves to be victims of reverse discrimination. The views of affirmative-action officers in higher education are offered in this section.

The final section answers the question, "Why bother?" Reasons include the fact that affirmative-action programs are needed since inequities continue, and that affirmative-action programs can be fair. The authors advocate affirmative action as a policy that can work, and they recommend ways to effectively and fairly design and implement affirmative-action programs. For example, they note that a prerequisite of effective affirmative-action programs is strong, public commitment from top management. These executives control resources, they are in charge of decision-making, and they can influence organizational norms. They also point out that one of the most important shortcomings of current affirmative-action policies is the failure to recognize that whites and men can also be hired, promoted, and terminated in ways that directly affect affirmative-action efforts.

These authors address the continuing debate about whether affirmative action works and whether diversity initiatives should incorporate affirmative-action models and methods. They conclude that affirmative action can play an important and effective role in any organization's attempts to develop its diverse work force, and that the agendas of affirmative action and diversity are compatible. Managers struggling to reconcile the two in their own diversity efforts are likely to find this information to be helpful.

❖❖❖

Catalyst. *Women in Corporate Management: Model Programs for Development and Mobility.* New York: Catalyst, 1991. 67 pages.

This report presents results from the third stage of an extensive Catalyst study on the status of female managers and professionals in corporate America. (A report on the first two stages is described under Step 1, page 17.) It is based on an analysis of "the environment and programs of seventeen companies that have initiated exemplary programs for developing and advancing women." The criteria used in this study and the types of model programs described, as well as the case studies included, can help managers understand and choose options for their own diversity effort.

Ten criteria were used to evaluate corporate initiatives: motivation, or a link to the business strategy; rationale, or how well the initiative was structured to achieve its goals; clear, measurable goals and objectives; champions in senior-line positions; financial commitment; communication to employees about the initiative's existence, goals, and relationship to other business objectives; accountability for managers to effectively manage human resources; measurable outcomes; targeting women as eligible participants; and the extent to which the initiative could be effectively replicated in other companies.

Step 3

The types of initiatives chosen as models fall into nine groups: programs for balancing work and family, programs to address corporate cultural/environmental barriers to women's development, leadership development/upward mobility programs, accountability programs, mentoring programs, managing diversity programs, corporate women's groups, programs to eliminate sexual harassment, and programs for women of color. Each type of initiative is discussed separately, including a definition and various options to consider when designing one. The reasons for the program are also discussed, and examples of different companies' approaches are described.

In the section on accountability programs, or programs that "use incentives to reward managers who achieve corporate goals" the options for female managers include simple, verbal recognition given in private during a performance review, public recognition via widely-circulated progress reports, or tying managers' bonuses to their progress. The rationale for accountability programs describes the quick results possible to achieve rapid change and their effectiveness in getting high-potential women the visibility and exposure they need early in their careers. The process used at The Prudential Insurance Co. of America is mentioned as an example, which involves annual, high-level staff inventory meetings and affirmative-action meetings. Another example given is Tenneco Corporation, which has modified its executive-compensation program and succession-planning process to better incorporate the company's goals for female managers.

Other programs described in this report as exemplary include those at American Airlines, Inc., AT&T, The Chubb Corp., Colgate-Palmolive Co., Connecticut Mutual Life Insurance Co., Corning Incorporated, DuPont, Fannie Mae, Honeywell Inc., John Hancock Financial Services, Procter & Gamble Co., S. C. Johnson & Son, Inc., U.S. Sprint, U.S. West, Inc., and Xerox Corporation. Some of these programs are not aimed exclusively at women, and it is possible that even those that are can be usefully applied to other nontraditional managers or to the work force as a whole. This book is a useful resource in assessing the kinds of practices that might fit into an organization's diversity effort.

Step 3

❖❖❖

Cox, Taylor, Jr. "The Multicultural Organization." *Academy of Management Executive* 5:2, May 1991, pp. 34-47.

This article describes the characteristics of a multi-cultural organization (distinguished from ones that are mono-lithic or plural) and the tools available to create change toward the multicultural model. Cox constructs a framework to analyze the extent of integration. It is based on the diversity initiatives of U.S. organizations and Milton Gordon's societal-integration model (*Assimilation in American Life,* Oxford University Press, 1964), which is comprised of six dimensions: acculturation, structural integration, informal integration, cultural bias, organizational identification, and intergroup conflict.

These six dimensions can be used to analyze organizations in terms of their stage of development on cultural diversity. For example, monolithic organizations are highly homogeneous, typically relegate women and "racioethnic minority" men to low-status jobs, and encourage assimilation of those different from the majority. Intergroup conflict is minimized due to the homogeneity, but discrimination and prejudice are prevalent. Plural organizations are more heterogeneous and inclusive of women and people of color, but they still rely on assimilation and fail to address cultural aspects of integration. Multicultural organizations, the most desirable form in this framework, are characterized by a pluralistic mode of acculturation, structural integration that includes active hiring and placement of non-majority employees, inclusion of minority-culture members in informal networks and activities outside of normal working hours, an absence of prejudice and discrimination, feelings of belonging, loyalty and commitment to the organization among non-majority members, and low levels of intergroup conflict.

The twenty-two tools described by the author for moving organizations toward multiculturalism fit into the six dimensions. Tools listed for achieving full structural integration are: education programs, affirmative-action programs, targeted career-development programs, changes in managerial performance appraisal and reward systems, and changes in human resource policies and benefits. Examples of these tools are given, along with names of companies using them. Cox notes Amtrak's practice of tying affirmative-action objectives to managers' promotions and compensation, and Exxon's practice of reviewing the career-development plans of at least ten non-traditional employees as part of each division manager's performance evaluation.

These descriptions of tools that can be used to move organizations toward multiculturalism are brief and leave many details to the imagination. There are, however, many ideas here for practitioners to pursue, along with potential corporate contacts and a structure to link the variety of tools available with key objectives in a diversity effort.

Step 3

Falkenberg, Loren. "Improving the Accuracy of Stereotypes Within the Workplace." *Journal of Management* 16:1, 1990, pp. 107-118.

In this article, Falkenberg treats stereotyping as a "neutral, necessary cognitive process" which, when inaccurate, leads to negative consequences for an organization (as in the case of gender stereotyping). Stereotypes are maintained in several ways. Falkenberg notes that "information that does not fit current perceptions is ignored," and that behavior inconsistent with expectations is attributed to luck or situational factors and is never expected again. He also points out that as the proportion of minority-group members increases in a group, they are perceived as more threatening to in-group members and viewed even more negatively.

Step 3

The author states that revising stereotypes is a slow process. Behavior that does not conform to expectations is attended to but not acted upon unless it continues and is exhibited by additional out-group members. As minority membership increases, considerable personal interaction between them and in-group members is needed to replace broad group stereotypes with expectations based on individual characteristics or other, more accurate group stereotypes (functional, occupational, etc.).

For these reasons, Falkenberg argues that "organizations must attempt to improve the flow of accurate information and intentionally structure the membership of work groups." When a promotion is announced, for example, management should provide the rationale in writing, including the individual's specific achievements related to the promotion, so that employees do not attribute the promotion to other stereotype-consistent reasons. This process is important to follow for individuals belonging to the in-group as well as those with minority status.

In integrating work groups, he suggests that management explain in writing the task and the various members' qualifications before a group meets, so that the in-group members do not depend on their stereotypes in responding to members with minority status. These and other suggestions for creating and structuring work groups are useful to help break down dysfunctional but strongly-held stereotypes based on sex, ethnicity, and other personal characteristics.

Despite the academic nature of this article, the implications for developing diversity in an organization come through clearly and are based on a solid theoretical foundation. This work is helpful in understanding the dynamics of "in groups" and "out groups" and how the stereotypes about out-group members can be changed over time.

Galinsky, Ellen, Dana E. Friedman, and Carol A. Hernandez. *The Corporate Reference Guide to Work-Family Programs.* New York: Families and Work Institute, 1991. 437 pages.

This reference book is designed to answer such important questions as: What are my competitors and other companies in my industry doing? How did they get started? What features make work-family programs most effective, and what pitfalls can be avoided? What is the cost of these programs, and which ones are likely to yield the greatest return on investment? The book includes a detailed chart of 172 companies by industry and there are tables throughout the text.

Step 3

The authors first describe the stages in the development of work-family programs, using a model based on survey data from 188 of the largest companies in 30 industries. Next, they introduce a benchmarking tool to compare a company's policies with others in terms of "family-friendliness." Case studies and comparison of the four "friendliest" companies (Johnson & Johnson, IBM, Aetna Life and Casualty Co., and Corning Incorporated) illustrate successful approaches, and an analysis of the 188 companies identifies the prevalence of work-family initiatives and the characteristics of family-friendly companies.

The authors review work-family research (including their impact on productivity), discuss the 76 most exemplary programs, and provide an extensive chart that profiles the work-family policies of 172 of the companies surveyed.

The benchmarking tool, The FWI Family-Friendly Index, is divided into seven major categories: flexible work arrangements; leaves; financial assistance; corporate giving/community service; dependent-care services; management change; and work-family stress management. Policies and programs are rated using six criteria: impact, coverage, institutionalization, commitment, level of effort, and innovativeness. Examples and explanations throughout the text make it possible for a company to effectively use this tool in comparing its initiatives with other companies.

Case studies of 76 model initiatives are divided into sections for easy referencing: program, history, obstacles, results, advice, and future. A contact person is also included. Nine themes that consistently emerge as key ingredients to the success of these initiatives are: Get management support, customize the program, visit other companies, keep it simple (especially in the beginning), always keep quality in mind, use expert consultants, clearly explain programs to managers and employees, appoint a coordinator, and track success.

This book is the classic reference on the topic of work-family practices in companies. It is sure to be useful to any organization serious about improving its work-family programs as part of a diversity effort.

A companion piece to this reference book is Dana Friedman's article, "Work and Family: The New Strategic Plan" in *Human Resource Planning* (Volume 13[2], 1990, pages 70-89). It reviews how corporations are responding to workers' family needs (child care, elder care, and flexible-work schedules) and some of the management beliefs that obstruct work-family initiatives ("presence equals performance," "hours equal output," "equity means the same," etc.).

Step 3

❖❖❖

Jamieson, David, and O'Mara, Julie. *Managing Workforce 2000: Gaining the Diversity Advantage* San Francisco: Jossey-Bass Inc., 1991. 241 pages.

This book's focus is on the "flex-management model"— how to create more individualized policies, systems, and management practices. This model requires changing the ways that people and jobs are matched, performance is managed and rewarded, people are informed and involved, and lifestyles and life needs are met and supported. The description of the model is supplemented with case study examples from eighty-two organizations which are attempting to use parts of this model to change their corporate culture. The authors emphasize the

importance of recognizing that equality does not mean same-
ness, and that appreciating differences is the necessary first
step towards implementing change.

The authors list five skills that they feel are the most
important skills managers should master to effectively manage
the changing work force. These include empowering others,
developing others, valuing diversity, working for change, and
communicating responsibility. They describe what each of the
skills involves and provide tips for developing managers defi-
cient in them. The authors advocate the use of Beckhard and
Harris's (*Organizational Transitions: Managing Complex
Changes* [2nd edition]; Addison-Wesley, 1987) six-step plan of
action for implementing change combined with their flex-
management model. The six steps include: defining the
organization's diversity, understanding the organization's
work-force values and needs, describing the desired future
state, analyzing the present state, planning and managing
transitions, and evaluating results.

These authors do not limit their discussion of the diverse *Step 3*
work force to people of color and white women. They examine
the important role that other nontraditional groups play in
organizations, including older workers, persons with disabili-
ties, and people with different values and educational backgrounds. Their emphasis is not on developing diversity in
upper management, but rather on how to get the most out of
the diverse employees currently in a company.

The strength of this book is that it describes a process to
make a corporate culture more agreeable and "friendly" to
people of diverse backgrounds and skills. Also, a resource
section listing sixty-five consultants, research centers, and
organizations that are available to help is particularly useful
for newcomers to this field.

❖❖❖

Sachs, Robert. "The Final Frontier of Competitive Advantage?"
    Business Forum, Spring 1990, pp. 5-7.

This article describes how organizations can use people to
gain a competitive edge by creating a healthy and productive
work environment. The author reviews a few of the methods

that can be used to attain this goal: improve the recruitment process to produce a better person-job match to reduce turnover and absenteeism; change the merit system to reward desirable organizational behavior; meet employees' needs by increasing flexibility in the benefits programs, reduce stress, and assist with family care; and improve communication between managers and their subordinates.

One strategy recommended for ensuring a better person-job match is to cast aside traditional job criteria such as previous experience, formal education, scholastic tests, and grade-point averages and use instead a process called "competency profiling" in conjunction with behavioral event interviews (BEIs). Competency profiling uses a panel of company experts to identify outstanding performance and the characteristics that contribute to it. These characteristics are then used as criteria in making productive person-job matches. BEIs are conducted with both top and average performers to substitute true behavioral descriptions for assumptions about what outstanding performers are doing, thinking, and feeling.

Step 3

The author explains that a Fortune 500 retailer used these methods successfully after realizing that 40% of the sales managers were leaving within six months of being hired. The expert panel (using the competency-based approach) identified the key characteristics of a successful sales manager to be extroverted, aggressive, customer-oriented, and to have a sense of humor. But the BEI revealed a very different success profile: Successful sales managers were highly energetic, time-conscious, able to set internal standards for their performance, spent their spare time in sales-related activities, were able to size up the probability of a sale quickly and accurately, followed up with customers as promised, and routinely provided extra service needed to close a sale. Using the BEI profile as the selection criteria, the retailer hired more sales managers who happened to be women and people with no sales background. After the first year of adopting this new hiring approach, sales were fifteen to twenty percent higher.

In the compensation area, some of the more innovative and effective reward systems being tried in companies in all levels of management are gainsharing, unit incentives, and key contributor programs. DuPont is one example of a company that has implemented a new incentive program called

"Achievement Sharing." Improved communication is also being used to enhance employee productivity. Confidential telephone surveys are being tried in some companies to keep management and employees informed of employee attitudes and to send a message to the employees that management cares.

This article provides stimulating ideas for managers to undertake in an organizational change effort. The examples are effective in describing the kind of change that can take place using the methods described.

Recruitment

Dickson, Reginald D. "The Business of Equal Opportunity." *Harvard Business Review,* January-February 1992, pp. 46-53.

Step 3

Dickson, President and CEO of Inroads Inc., begins this article with "I love the capitalist system." He describes his national organization which helps put talented young students of color into business and technology jobs. Inroads has been successfully used as a recruitment tool by many companies, and this article explains how the organization works. This work goes beyond recruitment, however, because Dickson also describes his own background and the philosophy behind Inroads, emphasizing the need for people of color to adapt to the dominant norms.

Dickson notes that the goal of Inroads is to identify the most capable high-school students of color who are interested in careers in business or technology and match them with corporate sponsors who will guide them through college and use them as interns, and—if the match is right—provide them with career employment when they graduate. Students must successfully complete a rigorous screening process and, once selected, they must dedicate four years of their lives to Inroads activities: community service on weekends, workshops and training sessions on Saturdays, summer internships with their sponsors, in addition to maintaining a B average in school. In return, Inroads promises them corporate sponsors who will pay them competitive salaries for summer internships, provide them with a mentor, and help them outline a career-development plan. Inroads charges corporations about $3,500 per year for each intern they sponsor.

The author emphasizes that Inroads is not an affirmative-action program. Its clients are the corporate employers, not the interns. Inroads encourages corporate self-interest, assuming that "the place of minorities in the corporate world has to be secure, and only corporate self-interest will make it so." Dickson's remarks about the responsibility of minority students to adapt and assimilate, and that the glass ceiling may be only in the minds of nontraditionals, provoked letters from a host of individuals in the private and public sectors. These letters were published as an article titled "Can equal opportunity be made more equal?" in the March-April issue of *HBR* (pages 138-158). They generally laud Inroads' success but question its premises, suggesting that the Inroads message to students is "overly optimistic" and that the best success recipe may not be "having the individual bear the adaptation burden alone."

Step 3

The issues raised in these two articles represent excellent material to use to stimulate discussion among task-force members in determining appropriate goals for a diversity effort or among executives in a training or orientation session.

Laabs, Jennifer J. "Affirmative Outreach." *Personnel Journal,* May 1991, pp. 86-93.

Using examples from the Department of Corrections, the IRS, and other organizations, Laabs shows how employers are shifting their emphasis from recruiting people of color, women, and people with different abilities (the affirmative-action approach) to recruiting a "sufficient number of qualified and quality employees regardless of ethnic characteristics." This article is meant to help organizations do this. One technique, for example, is to begin by diversifying the recruitment staff itself in order to add sensitivity and credibility to the recruitment effort.

Laabs describes the variety of recruitment methods used by the Department of Corrections: newspaper and magazine ads, and radio and television commercials; recruitment messages on posters and billboards; mailers and handouts; multimedia slide presentations; videos to community organizations; and job-information workshops in target communities. Also, the IRS has implemented a unique recruitment strategy which includes a high-school mentorship program, a curriculum-enhancement program for taxation and accounting, a service-wide strategic initiative aimed at increasing the recruitment and retention of women and people of color, and regular communication with college-placement offices across the U.S.

The author also includes warnings about some traditional recruiting methods—for one, ignoring recruits' developmental needs. Also, randomly selecting high schools or colleges as recruiting sources is not sufficient; choosing those with a high percentage of the targeted population will yield better results. And recruitment ads need to be carefully constructed because too much of an emphasis on recruiting people of color and women can be as harmful as no emphasis. "By putting too much emphasis on minority hiring in advertising, candidates may wonder what your goal is—to hire more [people of color] or to hire more individuals who have the skills you need." This article suggests that it is better to target your audience through the media, rather than through the message.

Step 3

Laabs presents basic recruitment approaches and identifies more innovative and sensitive strategies. This article cautions recruiters about mistakes made by others, and it demonstrates how recruitment strategies can be subtle and can still effectively reach a more diverse audience.

Lin, Thung-Rung, Gregory H. Dobbins, and Jiing-Lih Farh. "A Field Study of Race and Age Similarity Effects on Interview Ratings in Conventional and Situational Interviews." *Journal of Applied Psychology* 77:3, 1992, pp. 363-371.

This study investigates whether age or race similarity between interviewers and interviewees influences the outcome of selection interviews, and whether these factors were controlled by the type of interview used (structured panel interviews vs. situational panel interviews). It was expected that interview ratings would be more favorable when the interview panel was of the same race/same age as the interviewee, and that more same-age and same-race bias would occur with the conventional than with the situational interview.

Conventional structured interviews use questions developed on the basis of job analysis, ask the same questions of each candidate, have rating scales anchored with behaviors, use a panel to record and rate answers, have a consistent format administered to all candidates, and pay special attention to fairness in accordance with testing guidelines. Situational interviews use two interview forms with twenty situational questions: nine questions are identical on both forms and eleven questions are unique to each form.

Step 3

More than 2,700 custodian job applicants were divided into two groups—the first group was interviewed using a conventional structured interview, the second group was interviewed using a situational interview. In addition, each applicant was interviewed by one of three types of panels: a same-race panel with both interviewers of the same race as the interviewee, a mixed-race panel with only one interviewer of the same race as the interviewee, and a different-race panel with both interviewers of different races from that of the interviewee. Panels were further grouped as same-age, mixed-age, or different-age using four age groups: under 25 years old, 25 to 35, 35 to 45, and over 45. The design of this study solves some problems with previous interview bias studies; it examines same-race bias in a field-interview setting (instead of in a simulation); and it includes Hispanics as well as blacks and whites.

Results for the structured interview panels show that black/black panels rated black applicants more favorably than did black/other and other/other panels. Similarly, Hispanic/Hispanic panels rated Hispanic applicants more favorably than did Hispanic/other or other/other panels. Surprisingly, white/white panels evaluated whites as less qualified than did other/other panels.

The situational interview panels, which showed much less same-race bias than the structured interviews, only indicated one difference among the three types of panels: the black/black panels rated black interviewees more favorably than did other/

other panels. Interviewer race had no impact on Hispanic or white interviewees' scores. Also, no significant same-age bias was found in either the structured or the situational interviews.

This study supports the use of mixed-race panels for interviewing applicants. It also suggests that less same-race bias may occur in situational interviews than in structural interviews. While more research should be done on this topic with higher-level applicants, this study offers persuasive suggestions about how to create less biased interview panels.

Development

Ilgen, Daniel R., and Margaret A. Youtz. "Factors Affecting the Evaluation and Development of Minorities in Organizations." In *Performance Evaluation, Goal Setting, and Feedback*. Gerald R. Ferris and Kendrith M. Rowland, eds. Greenwich, CT: JAI Press Inc., 1990, pp. 261-293.

Step 3

This article connects career-development activities with the dynamics of performance and how it is evaluated in many organizations. The authors explain how some development practices such as mentoring and job assignments relate to managers' actual and perceived job performance and the kinds of cycles that may improve or limit performance among people of color.

The authors summarize a number of studies showing lower performance ratings for people of color compared with whites, and they discuss a number of possible causes of this. Rater bias is one factor, which comes from stereotyping, attributing reasons to others' performance, or using only selected information that confirms one's expectations. Another possibility is the effect of fewer or less favorable on-the-job opportunities for people of color, such as the absence of mentors, sponsors, and role models, less exciting work assignments as a member of the "out group," and exclusion from social networks. While these lost opportunities may not directly affect performance ratings, they may over time contribute to limited performance. A combined, long-term effect of experiencing rating biases and lost opportunities may be self-limiting behavior by people of color that occurs unconsciously.

The courses of action recommended by the authors are directed toward two interactive components. One is the evaluation of people of color, which is more typically done in organizations, and the other is the treatment of people of color which contributes to minority/majority performance differences. The authors argue that training managers to eliminate common rating errors, for example, may not be as effective as training geared to improve rating accuracy or training that focuses specifically on problems of rating people of color. They also argue for more attention to career-development activities, such as more effective social integration of newcomers and building mentoring programs that may involve using psychological testing in matching mentors and protégés.

Step 3

Many of the suggested actions appear in more sophisticated forms in other works. The value of this article is in the connections made between how personal performance interacts with one's access, treatment, and other working conditions. The implications for career development for nontraditional managers are related to other management practices and the person-situation dynamics that occur in organizations.

❖❖❖

Kakabadse, Andrew, and Charles Margerison. "The Female Chief Executive: An Analysis of Career Progress and Development Needs." *Journal of Managerial Psychology* 2:2, 1987, pp. 17-25.

Although one year older than our 1988 cutoff date, this is the only research we could find comparing female and male CEOs. The authors investigated how women attain the level of CEO and compare the results with their earlier study of male CEOs. Their findings, based on survey data from twenty-nine female U.S. company CEOs and interviews with another six female CEOs in the U.K., suggest some areas in which the career experience of women might be improved.

The female CEOs studied tended to enter upper management at an earlier age than their male counterparts (about two years younger), attained the position of CEO at an earlier age (about six years younger), and had fewer years of management experience. They also tended to have more education and to have worked for more companies than their male counterparts.

Factors important in the career development of the women were dominated by personal drive characteristics—a need to achieve results, willingness to take risks, challenge, etc. Two other types of characteristics ranked lower—interpersonal skills and exposure to a width of business experience. The male CEOs in the prior study identified the same characteristic as the most important influence on their success—a need to achieve results—but they tended to put greater emphasis on a width of business experience. Also, concerning interpersonal skills, most women rated "developing and using political skills in the organisation" as a key factor, but the men tended to consider this "an undesirable aspect of organisational life."

When asked about the most important things they had to learn to perform as an executive, women and men responded somewhat differently. Female CEOs emphasized achieving results by concentrating on tasks rather than by working in teams, whereas the men indicated a greater preference for working in teams to achieve results. Also, the women ranked self-discipline and analytical abilities as the most important personal activities; men ranked strategic planning and decision-making highest.

Both women and men cited ambition as their overriding reasons for reaching the top, but women indicated that self-oriented characteristics such as talent, foresight, planning, and risk-taking led to their success. Male CEOs, in contrast, identified leadership abilities and interpersonal skills as more important success determinants.

The authors offer possible explanations for the differences and four conclusions about the management-development experiences that need to be offered to women in the areas of identifying and encouraging managerial potential, developing skill in managing people, using management education programs to complement on-the-job experience, and allocating time for personal development. Because these findings contradict some common beliefs about female and male executives,

Step 3

this research may help managers view career development in a
different light.

Nkomo, Stella M., and Taylor Cox, Jr. "Gender Differences
      in the Upward Mobility of Black Managers: Double
      Whammy or Double Advantage?" *Sex Roles* 21, 1989,
      pp. 825-839.

These researchers note the dearth of research on black
women in management and question whether black women can
be lumped together with white women or with black men to
determine factors important in their career mobility. Their
results, which show some significant differences between black
women and men in management, suggest that career-planning
activities in a diversity effort should take into account the sex
of the managers to be developed.

Step 3

The researchers surveyed 283 male and female managers
belonging to the National Black MBA Association to determine
whether black women or men had a higher rate of upward
mobility. Biographical information and responses related to six
mobility factors showed different predictors of upward mobility
for black female and male managers. For the women, the size
of the organization, the percent of black employees, mentor
help, and job involvement were more important to their advancement. That is, black women "advance better in large
organizations where they have some mentor help." More important for the men were the frequency of management vacancies,
the number of management levels, the extent of equal employment opportunity/affirmative action, line assignments, and
their interracial social activity.

This study counters the assumption that black women
experience a double whammy or a double advantage (as a "two-
fer"), and highlights the need to take into account both sex and
ethnicity in examining barriers to advancement and designing
potential solutions. The six mobility factors used in this study
may also be useful in developing an internal investigation and
in constructing developmental activities.

Van Velsor, Ellen, and Martha W. Hughes. *Gender Differences in the Development of Managers: How Women Managers Learn From Experience.* Greensboro, NC: Center for Creative Leadership, 1990. 121 pages.

This research report examines why women have not advanced to executive-level positions: Do women have less opportunity to develop, especially on the job? Alternatively, do women's learning patterns differ from men's, so that they develop in unexpected ways from the same experiences? These questions are important in creating a developmental strategy for nontraditional managers in organizations.

The authors analyze data from 78 female executives and 189 male executives from large corporations. This information—about the key events and lessons that helped them develop as executives—was originally collected and used in three other publications: *Breaking the Glass Ceiling* (Morrison, White, and Van Velsor, 1987 [updated in 1992]; Addison-Wesley), *Key Events in Executives' Lives* (Lindsey, Homes, and McCall, 1987; Center for Creative Leadership), and *The Lessons of Experience* (McCall, Lombardo, and Morrison, 1988; Lexington Books). An extensive appendix includes specific data comparing women's and men's reported lessons and the sources of those lessons.

Step 3

The analysis shows that male executives attributed more of their lessons to on-the-job assignments such as promotions, task forces, start-ups, and troubleshooting than did their female counterparts (60% of men's lessons compared with 43% for women). Women reported learning more lessons from other people, particularly their bosses, than did men (28% of women's lessons compared with 14% for men). The authors suggest that these learning patterns may differ because women receive fewer opportunities to experience, and thus learn from, certain assignments. None of the female executives studied, for example, reported a start-up assignment as a key event, compared with 17% of the male executives. Also, 30% of the men reported a turnaround assignment as a key event in their development, compared with only 6% of the women. The authors contend that reluctance to give female managers these kinds of key assignments may limit their learning.

The authors also discovered that the types of lessons are somewhat different for female and male executives. Though both men and women frequently reported learning self-confidence and lessons about directing and motivating employees, basic management values, how to work with executives, and so on, women more frequently learned about personal limits and blind spots, taking charge of your career, recognizing and seizing opportunities, coping with situations beyond your control, and knowing what excites you. Men more frequently reported lessons about technical and professional skills, all about the business, coping with ambiguous situations, shouldering full responsibility, and persevering through adversity.

It is not clear whether these sex differences in learning patterns are due to different learning sources (assignments versus other people, for example) or to different learning predispositions. The authors do note, however, that assignments and other learning situations that appear to be comparable for women and men may in fact differ significantly because of the greater visibility of female managers and the demands that their unique status as pioneers make on them. They call for providing developmental opportunities that provide both adequate challenge and ample support for female managers to help overcome barriers to their advancement.

Step 3

These researchers, like Joan V. Gallos ("Exploring Women's Development: Implications for Career Theory, Practice, and Research" in *Handbook of Career Theory,* New York, Cambridge University Press, 1989), raise crucial points about the developmental process, needs, and learning patterns of women. Although they do not provide a model for developing female or other nontraditional managers, their research findings are helpful in developing both a model and tools to foster the development of diversity in organizations.

Mentoring

Burke, Ronald, and Carol A. McKeen. "Developing Formal Mentoring Programs in Organizations." *Business Quarterly* 53:3, Winter 1989, pp. 76-79.

This article highlights questions that should be asked when establishing a formal-mentoring program and anticipating the problems that can arise. The value of mentoring is commonly acknowledged, but the effectiveness of formal-mentoring programs is regularly debated. These authors tie mentoring to career development and reduced turnover, and they devote considerable attention to how a mentoring program must be designed to achieve these goals. They mention how education can encourage effective mentoring relationships, along with structural change to modify the organization's reward systems, tasks, and performance-appraisal process. They also portray one mentoring program in which the mentor is two levels higher in the hierarchy than the protégés and consults with the reporting manager.

Step 3

Questions about whether participation in the program should be voluntary or mandatory, and how mentors and protégés will be assigned, are brought out. Potential problems are also alluded to, such as the complexities of male-female mentoring relationships, dealing with managers not chosen as mentors, and the sometimes difficult job of blending the efforts of the protégé, the mentor, and the protégé's boss and boss's boss.

As an overview, this article is a prelude to continued thought and reading on the subject. It alerts managers to several significant aspects of mentoring programs, which will help determine whether and how to pursue such a program. Other resources are needed to answer the questions raised.

Kizilos, Peter. "Take My Mentor, Please!" *Training,* April 1990, pp. 49-55.

The assertion that mentoring is a requirement for a successful career is dismissed in this article. Although the author recognizes that mentoring has helped some succeed, he does not see it as mandatory to success. Some of the arguments for and against formal-mentoring programs are discussed, with a final conclusion that many organizations use formal-mentoring programs as a quick fix to problems instead of doing the hard work of changing the corporate culture. Many managers feel that if they have a mentoring program in place, they don't need to worry about the deep-seated problems such as the performance-appraisal system and the reward system.

The author leads up to this conclusion by presenting opponents' and proponents' arguments. Many of the opponents to formal-mentoring programs downplay the significance of mentoring relationships in general and of formal programs in particular. They argue that true mentor-protégé relationships must evolve naturally. And these critics argue that formal-mentoring programs may cause more problems than they solve. Forced coupling can fuel discontent, anger, resentment and suspicion. Not all managers are ready to take on a mentoring role. Often designers of formal-mentoring programs make the mistake of using as mentors "old-timers" who are no longer contributing to the everyday success of the organization. These managers are often threatened by the new fast-track protégé, and they can sabotage the relationship or the protégé's career. Other problems can arise even with successful relationships, particularly if the relationship lasts too long and there is no formal transition process out of the mentor-protégé relationship. This situation can lead to resentment by both participants.

In addition to these problems with formal-mentoring programs in general, additional problems arise in cross-sex relationships. Kizilos argues that stylistic differences between male mentors and female protégés can create misunderstandings that lead the mentor to conclude that the protégé can't manage conflicts or difficult situations simply because she doesn't handle them the way he would.

Proponents of mentoring programs argue that teaming new employees with mentors can help train them and help them learn the organizational norms. They argue that managers with mentors are happier with their career progress and take more pleasure from their work.

Although this article seems biased against formal-mentoring programs, even strong advocates of these programs should consider the opponents' arguments if only to avoid some of the pitfalls that can hurt them.

❖❖❖

Kram, Kathy E. *Mentoring at Work: Developmental Relationships in Organizational Life.* Lanham, MD: University Press of America, Inc., 1988. 252 pages.

In Kram's words, this book provides "a thorough understanding of the psychological and organizational factors which facilitate supportive relationships," and suggests "specific strategies for enhancing the quality of worklife and career development practices of their organization."

Kram's four phases of the mentor relationship have been recognized as a valuable conceptual framework by many authors and practitioners. These four phases are: initiation, cultivation, separation, and redefinition. During the initiation phase (six months to a year), both the protégé and the senior-manager mentor develop "fantasies" about the other. The protégé fantasizes about being protected and supported; the mentor fantasizes about the potential in the young manager to be an object for the transmission of the senior manager's values and perspectives of the world. The cultivation phase (two to five years) tests and retests the reality of the fantasies, and the real value of the relationship becomes apparent. Then, separation occurs after about two to five years and involves feelings of turmoil, anxiety, and loss as "the equilibrium of the cultivation phase is disrupted." Both managers reassess the value of the relationship. The young manager experiences more independence and autonomy, and the mentoring relationship becomes a less central part of their worklife. Redefinition occurs after several years of separation, once the stress of the separation diminishes and the relationship takes on a new meaning and role in both managers' lives.

Kram outlines the career and psychosocial functions of the mentor. Understanding these is crucial to recognizing the benefits that both the protégé and mentor get from the rela-

Step 3

tionship. The career functions are: sponsorship, exposure and visibility, coaching, protection, and challenging assignments. The psychosocial functions are: role modeling, acceptance and confirmation, counseling, and friendship.

She also investigates the complexities of cross-sex relationships and describes five problems that women face in cross-sex mentoring: collusion in stereotypical roles, limitations of the mentor providing an accurate role model due to sex differences, intimacy and sexuality concerns, public scrutiny, and peer resentment. Alternatives to mentoring consist of peer relationships which also satisfy career and psychosocial needs. The career functions of peer relationships include: information sharing, career strategizing, and job-related feedback. The psychosocial functions of peer relationships include: confirmation, emotional support, personal feedback, and friendship. Though the mentoring relationship can be seen as complementary, the peer relationship can be viewed as mutual.

A chapter on "Creating Conditions That Encourage Mentoring" includes a discussion of structural changes to make an organizational climate more conducive to mentoring, including changing the reward system, performance-management systems, or the design of work.

Step 3

This book is frequently quoted and referenced by many researchers studying mentoring. It is not a "how-to" book like the one by Murray and Owen (this section, page 80), but it can be an important resource for managers who want to build more mentoring activities into their organizations.

❖❖❖

Kram, Kathy E., and Madeline C. Bragar. "Development Through Mentoring: A Strategic Approach." In *Career Development: Theory and Practice* by D. Montross and C. Shinkman, eds. Chicago, IL: Charles C. Thomas, 1992, pp. 221-254.

Kram and Bragar demonstrate in this chapter that formal-mentoring programs represent only one alternative to developing people, one with considerable limitations. A strategic approach to improving mentoring is presented as a viable alternative to traditional formal-mentoring programs. The strategic approach takes into account current and future work-force needs and considers other human resources practices.

The authors identify a number of components which are core to a formal-mentoring program's effectiveness. For example, the target population and benefits to them should be identified, the selection process and matching system should be voluntary, orientation and training should be provided, and the program should be monitored and evaluated. In addition, these components must be included in the design in a manner that maximizes effectiveness rather than expediency, despite the current organizational climate of cost-cutting and downsizing.

Limitations to formal programs, though, may negate some benefits that the programs could otherwise supply. For example, the number of participants in a formal program is necessarily limited, so the costs to the organization might outweigh the benefits. Also, relationships which are developed through planned programs are often superficial. The authors claim that a more strategic approach which attempts to counter some of these limitations would strengthen the benefits to participants and to the organization.

Step 3

A strategic approach to mentoring programs would link the program to strategic business concerns and would therefore take a long-term perspective, would identify work-force requirements in terms of skill mix and learning needs, and would be organized around critical business issues such as quality or productivity. Methods of aligning mentoring programs with strategic business needs, of assessing the impact of current practices, of identifying and choosing alternatives, and of monitoring and evaluating the initiative are provided. An example provided of how it can benefit the organization to link mentoring programs to business needs is: "after the stock market crash in 1987, Merrill Lynch's Advanced Office Systems Group designed a career mentoring program to help leverage staff skills and training, to provide support in positioning staff for realistic success, and to retain valued staff who would otherwise search for career opportunities in non-downsizing corporations."

This chapter can help guide organizations to design effective mentoring programs and can help them prevent wasting resources. Economic conditions require practitioners to carefully evaluate how their organizations spend time and money, and this article demonstrates ways to get the most out of mentoring programs.

Murray, Margo, and Marna A. Owen. *Beyond the Myths and Magic of Mentoring: How to Facilitate an Effective Mentoring Program.* San Francisco: Jossey-Bass Inc., 1991. 210 pages.

This practical "how-to" book presents arguments for winning top management's commitment to mentoring, offers models for successful mentoring programs, and provides practical steps for designing a mentoring program. It is conveniently organized to allow practitioners to skip to the chapters most relevant to their needs.

Part I explains how to assess whether a mentoring program will help your organization and offers information about how to persuade top management that a mentoring program will benefit the participants and the organization. Some of the reasons other companies have implemented mentoring programs are: the need for leadership, the awareness of the needs of an increasingly diverse work force, recognition of the changes caused by restructuring companies and the economy, and the need for succession planning and management development. Benefits and pitfalls for the organization, protégé, and mentor are all detailed in three separate chapters.

In Part II, seven different models of formal-mentoring programs are presented. The models include a generic model developed by Murray-Hicks (*Generic Model for a Facilitated Mentoring Program,* MMHA, 1972) and the mentoring program at the U.S. General Accounting Office. Flow-chart illustrations of each of these models are given, with a description of each of the steps involved in the model.

Murray offers methods to assess needs and determine an organization's readiness. This process includes determining the organization's future succession-planning needs, examining the organization's commitment to human resource development, determining the scope of the mentoring program, and assessing the organization's ability to sustain the characteristics of successful mentoring programs.

Step 3

Other chapters provide information on how to recruit, select, and reward mentors, how to select protégés and diagnose their developmental needs, how to involve the boss who is not the mentor, how to select and train the coordinator, what the coordinator's responsibilities are, how to negotiate sound mentoring agreements, and how to evaluate program effectiveness.

The final chapter is dedicated to an examination of gender, culture, and relationship concerns. Guidelines for handling potential problems arising from personal attraction are offered. For example, Murray recommends that the potential for sexual attraction be acknowledged and managed; the organization's policy on sexual harassment, homosexuality, dating other employees, and employment of related persons be discussed; and taboo relationships should be specified. Guidelines for handling potential problems with cross-cultural issues are also suggested. They include: Study the culture of those with whom you work and pay particular attention to the similarities and differences of individuals; expect just as much of members of other ethnic groups as you expect of members of your own; confront racism when it comes up and deal with it honestly.

Step 3

This book offers managers a variety of options for mentoring programs. Also, the checklists, worksheets, outlines, examples, and other tools help design effective mentoring programs and help ensure that each of the issues raised is confronted early in the design stages. Overall, this book provides a wealth of information for creating and running a mentoring program.

Awareness Training

Gentile, Mary C. "The Case of the Unequal Opportunity." *Harvard Business Review,* July-August 1991, pp. 14-25.

This *HBR* case study looks at the question of whether it is always wrong to consider gender, race, and ethnicity as factors in a promotion decision—even if the "equal" opportunity might end a manager's career. The case describes a situation in which a marketing director, Laura Wollen, must recommend a manager from her division for promotion to an assignment in the

United Kingdom. The two contenders for the assignment are Frank Billings (a white man) and Charles Lewis (a black man). Wollen believes that Lewis would be the better candidate for a variety of reasons. And David Abbott, Wollen's counterpart in the United Kingdom, sounds excited about her recommendation—until he learns that Lewis is black. His enthusiasm evaporates; he becomes angry that Wollen didn't alert him to Lewis's race, and wary about hiring Lewis. His concern is that Lewis won't be able to "fit in" with the British culture. Regardless of Wollen's persuasive arguments to the contrary, Abbott is convinced that Lewis will fail. Wollen faces the challenge of deciding what is best for the company, for Lewis, and for her.

Four experts on international management discuss this dilemma: Jim Kaiser of Corning Incorporated, Jeffalyn Johnson of the University of North Florida in Jacksonville, Brian Harvey of Nottingham University, Nottingham, England, and Nancy Adler of McGill University, Montreal, Canada. Three of the experts agree that Lewis should be given the overseas assignments; the fourth recommends only that Wollen level with Lewis. The reasons and methods for dealing with the issue are different, though, and both the problem and the answers can be used to provoke an interesting debate. Issues that arise in the expert answers are: The greatest barrier to overseas assignments is being American, not being black; make the decision work; do not protect people from failure; level with Lewis but don't make the decision for him; and don't let myths influence your decision.

It would have been interesting to read an argument that Lewis should not be given the position, because it would have provided more contrast to the others' arguments. This case study is a useful tool for soliciting views on how to handle diversity issues and would be a good way to begin a "valuing" or "managing-diversity" program. The study could be used alone or with the expert opinions. It could also be expanded in various ways and perhaps include role-playing.

Step 3

❖❖❖

Hacker, Andrew. "If You Were Born Black . . ." *Across the Board,* June 1992, pp. 34-39.

Hacker effectively demonstrates through stories and emotion-laden statements that black Americans already know what skin color means but white Americans "still don't get it." He points out that white people seldom stop to ask themselves how they may benefit from belonging to their race, and illustrates this through a parable that has been told to many students: An official visits you (a white person) tonight and tells you his organization has made a terrible mistake; you were supposed to have been born black, to another set of parents, far from where you were raised. He explains that this error must be corrected immediately, so at midnight tonight you will become black. You will have darker skin and the bodily and facial features associated with African ancestry. But inside you will be the same person. Your knowledge and personality will be the same but you will not be recognized by anyone you know. He informs you that his organization is wealthy and recognizes the inconvenience involved in this change. He stresses that they are willing to compensate you for this and asks you to state a sum of money that you feel is reasonable. He adds that you will live as a black man or woman for another fifty years. The most frequently mentioned sum of money that white students suggest as fair recompense is fifty million dollars, or one million dollars for each year as a black person. This serves to illustrate the value that whites put on their skin without realizing it.

Step 3

Hacker continues the article with thoughts and feelings that many black people have about life today in the United States. He intersperses this with pointed statistics such as, "white residents will stay [in a neighborhood]—and some new ones may move in—if black arrivals do not exceed eight percent. But once the black proportion passes that point, whites begin to leave the neighborhood and no new ones will move in."

The author's other reflections on being black or being white in the United States serve to show just how much discrimination and disparate treatment still exists in the U.S. today. For example, "the police are coming" evokes very different emotions in a white person than a black person.

This article helps explain to whites (and anyone else) why "they" are so angry. Although the "they" in this article are blacks, other people of color may relate to the examples and feelings revealed in this emotional yet reflective article. It is a useful tool for awareness training.

Johnson, Ronita B., and Julie O'Mara. "Shedding New Light on Diversity Training." *Training & Development,* May 1992, pp. 45-52.

This article describes why and how Pacific Gas & Electric (PG&E) trained and certified one hundred ten line and staff employees as diversity-awareness trainers by requiring them to participate in the train-the-trainer program. The company took this action to improve its competitive advantage in productivity, customer service, employee recruitment, and employee retention in a cost-effective manner and to diversify the work force.

Step 3

The train-the-trainer program lasts six days and consists of four phases. Four key behaviors (self-knowledge, leadership, subject-matter understanding and expertise, and facilitation skills) are identified as helpful in measuring the effectiveness of diversity-awareness trainers, and each trainee completes three self-assessments on these four behaviors to determine their progress on the behaviors. The assessments are done on the first, fifth, and sixth days of training.

Phase 1 includes self-assessment and a general-information session to educate the trainees about what to expect from the training and what to expect once they become trainers. Phase 2 is the beginning of a sixty-hour intensive train-the-trainer workshop. The trainees must read two books and then deal with their own stereotypes, biases, and assumptions. Feedback and coaching is woven into these sessions. The trainees practice as trainers and receive feedback from other trainees and trainers about their strengths, weaknesses, and effectiveness. In Phase 3, trainees conduct sessions with their actual business units or regions. Again, the trainees are observed and coached during this process. During Phase 4, qualified trainees receive certification and feedback on their use of the four competencies. The staff writes a report on each trainee's skill and ability to facilitate diversity-awareness training.

The train-the-trainer workshop is only one aspect of PG&E's commitment to diversity. Other elements of the diversity initiative are described as well. For example, PG&E's customer-service program helps eliminate language barriers and helps fashion the delivery of customer service to people of different ethnic groups.

Some benefits of internal trainers are outlined. For example, internal trainers can easily follow up with additional sessions and extra organizational work. Using internal trainers may also be more cost and time effective than hiring outside consultants. Managers will want to consider other factors as well, such as employees' confidentiality and fear of repercussions, and the accountability of managers. This article helps make decisions about whom to select for such a training effort and how to make the training effective.

Step 3

McIntosh, Peggy. *White Privilege and Male Privilege: A Personal Account of Coming to See Correspondences Through Work in Women's Studies.* Working Paper No. 189. Wellesley, MA: Wellesley College, Center for Research on Women, 1988. ©Peggy McIntosh. 20 pages.

"I think whites are carefully taught not to recognize white privilege," McIntosh writes, "as males are taught not to recognize male privilege. So I have begun in an untutored way to ask what it is like to have white privilege."

In this paper, McIntosh describes the process by which she came to recognize unearned overadvantage with regard to race, which she compares with the unearned overadvantage men enjoy in our society by virtue of their sex. She details forty-six ordinary and daily ways in which she experiences having white privilege in contrast to black colleagues in the same building and the same line of work.

McIntosh offers insight into unearned privilege and how it affects oneself and others. She identifies three forms: entitlements that all members of society ideally should have, unearned advantage that harms those who currently have it by giving them "license to be ignorant, oblivious, arrogant and destructive," and privileges that are a simple function of being a member of a numerical majority in the population. McIntosh reviews layers of denial that protect whites and males, demonstrating the similarities between what she has experienced from men and what she experiences as a white person.

Some of the many privileges of being white that McIntosh lists are: "I can, if I wish, arrange to be in the company of people of my race most of the time; I can be pretty sure that my neighbors will be neutral or pleasant to me on a day when I move into housing which I have chosen; I can turn on the television or open to the front page of the paper and see people of my race widely and positively represented; I am never asked to speak for all the people of my racial group; I can do well in a challenging situation without being called a credit to my race; I can be late to a meeting without having the lateness reflect on my race; I can choose blemish cover or bandages in 'flesh' color and have them more or less match my skin."

Step 3

McIntosh surfaces issues, through her personal account of an evolving awareness of racial and sexual advantage, that are central to a diversity effort. Her list of white privileges could be an effective way to open a session designed to raise managers' awareness. The author's analysis also provides a framework for developing an internal investigation or designing a training program.

Thiederman, Sondra. *Bridging Cultural Barriers For Corporate Success.* Lexington, MA: Lexington Books, 1991. 256 pages.

This book provides practitioners with training approaches, content, and exercises for teaching cross-cultural management techniques to managers. It is targeted to human resource professionals, managers, and employees who are trying to understand, supervise, and improve work relations with employees of diverse ethnic and racial backgrounds. Thiederman addresses such issues as how to eliminate communication problems resulting from accent or language barriers, how to better motivate a diverse work force, and how to more accurately evaluate culturally diverse applicants. Exercises provided throughout the book may be completed by the reader or incorporated into training programs to heighten awareness and stimulate discussion among participants.

The first four chapters cover topics that are typically discussed in diversity-awareness training, such as understanding and overcoming stereotypes, dealing with communication difficulties, and understanding differences in cultural values and styles. Vignettes related to language diversity and other issues are included with optional responses and an explanation of which options are better than others. Exercises to identify and correct the use of slang are also included. In the chapter on etiquette and style, an exercise on "finding your etiquette pet peeves" notes preferences for degree of formality, physical distance, vagueness of answers to questions, and so on.

Chapter five focuses on ways to motivate employees to change, such as how to overcome their fear and defensiveness and how to encourage them to take initiative and to bring problems to your attention. Thiederman advises managers to learn to speak key phrases of the worker's language, to learn methods of reinforcing desired behaviors, and to learn to interpret behavior correctly. Common phrases in thirteen languages are provided.

Step 3

The final chapter covers techniques and pitfalls in cross-cultural management training, with information on choosing content, format, and exercises, along with techniques for overcoming managers' resistance to training. One interesting exercise in the appendix suitable for a training program is a list of "cultural contrasts" that compares the U.S. with other cultures on such dimensions as control vs. fatalism, change vs. tradition, and becoming vs. being.

In another 1991 book, titled *Profiting in America's Multicultural Marketplace: How to Do Business Across Cultural Lines*, Thiederman includes some of the same content but directs it more specifically toward business managers and professionals who need to work with culturally different customers and associates. One chapter, for example, is on "cross-cultural customer service and sales." This book also contains exercises and summaries useful for training sessions, including a "cultural IQ" quiz likely to challenge many readers.

Both of these books offer practical content and tools to aid understanding of cultural differences, which can be used in training situations and in general.

Work, John W. *Toward Affirmative Action and Racial/Ethnic Pluralism: How to Train in Organizations.* Arlington, VA: Belvedere Press, 1989. 140 pages.

This handbook describes the process that trainers should use to prepare for affirmative-action training and the process of designing and implementing a diversity-training program. The difference between emotion-neutral, emotion-positive, and emotion-negative training is described. Diversity training is defined as emotion-negative due to its intent to "counter established and institutionalized social and personal values." Emotion-negative training requires the use of provocation to aid in the "unfreezing" of socialized values. Provocation can be done through the use of readings, audiovisuals, role-playing, case studies, and exercises combined with the use of provocative questions intended to induce a negative reaction (such as defensiveness, fear, anger, or denial).

Step 3

The author discusses certain problems that trainers can encounter when dealing with a negatively emotionally charged subject such as diversity. One problem trainers might face is the necessity to define terms such as racism and bigotry; they risk losing credibility if this is not done. Other added criteria for emotion-negative training are: The trainer must be committed to the intended change or the training will not be successful; the trainer must acquire additional knowledge of the history, manifestations, and subtleties of institutional racism; the trainer must be willing to provoke, challenge and criticize participants; and the trainer must be more flexible than when using emotion-neutral or emotion-positive training.

The objectives of the training session need to be clearly defined during the design stages. Elements that can be included in the training to achieve various objectives are described, and suggestions for each segment are offered. Sections to include in the training are: ice-breakers to release some of the tension built up from the announcement and commencement of an emotion-negative training program; climate setting to encourage participant identification with the theme of the training; a mini-lecture followed by a visual aid such as a film to begin narrowing the focus of the training; case studies to help with participant application of training to the real world; and, finally, barriers to be identified and plans for change to be developed. To aid the trainer, this book provides sample lectures, suggested films, examples of slides that could be used, sample case studies that could be incorporated, and a partial bibliography of suggested readings.

This book could be a valuable resource to a trainer, particularly one who has never done this type of emotionally charged training. Although no book can be complete, this one covers much more information than many longer books. It is clear and to the point, and it quickly allows the trainer to start designing a program.

Step 3

Accountability

Alderfer, Clayton P., Robert C. Tucker, Charleen J. Alderfer, and Leota M. Tucker. "The Race Relations Advisory Group: An Intergroup Intervention." *Research in Organizational Change and Development* 2, 1988, pp. 269-321.

The authors trace the history of an integrated advisory group in the fictitiously-named XYZ Corporation, noting how this group evolved over time and documenting the hurdles encountered by members over a seven-year period. This narrative reveals the complex dynamics that occur in a group torn between advising and confronting senior management and the role it plays as an organizational change agent.

The Race Relations Advisory Group, formed to help implement recommendations from a race-relations investigation within the corporation, began as a twelve-member group balanced by race and sex and representing various functional groups. It grew to twenty members after the investigation was completed, with nine of the original members remaining. This group worked closely with a four-member consulting team, also mixed by sex and race. The group met roughly bimonthly over the seven years of the project and went through four distinct phases: start-up, major intervention, crisis and realignment, and stabilization.

This group is one model for a long-term task force involved in designing key accountability tools and carrying out development activities in a diversity effort. It debated the issue of whether to limit the corporation's upward mobility program to blacks and dealt with top management's rejection of its recommendation. It also interfaced with the corporation's Black Managers' Association and helped develop a workshop of race-relations competency (described by Alderfer and his colleagues under Step 4, page 92) which they conducted for members of the corporation's board of directors.

An analysis of group members' behavior and attitudes, based on questionnaires completed periodically, shows the kinds of learning experienced by members and their perceptions of race relations over time. This section is sketchy and *Step 3* technical, and the findings may not be very useful. The value of this work is in revealing the polarizing issues that arise in a task force or employee group, the dynamics among group members, and the contributions that such a group can make to the organization's overall diversity effort. Anyone involved with employee advocacy groups is likely to find this journalistic account intriguing.

Step 4...

DEMAND RESULTS AND
REVISIT GOALS

The emphasis put on results may separate organizations that succeed in their diversity efforts from the field of hopefuls. When revenue or profit is a goal of a business function, progress is regularly measured and managers are held accountable for the results. When quality improvement or customer service is a goal, measures are devised to indicate progress, and managers are evaluated against them. When it comes to diversity, however, there is strong resistance to establishing indicators of progress and holding managers accountable for measurable results. This seems to be a major reason that many organizational efforts do not succeed.

How to measure progress on developing diversity is probably the most emotionally debated aspect of this issue. Adopting sensible measures—both quantitative and qualitative—is necessary to overcome strong resistance to focusing on concrete outcomes. Very little literature addresses this challenge, and so this step has fewer references than most. Those that are included describe ways to set realistic numerical goals, based on the costs of differential treatment and other factors. Profitability and productivity measures are included in some of these works. Also, ways to evaluate diversity practices such as training are covered.

Step 4

Alderfer, Clayton P., Charleen J. Alderfer, Ella L. Bell, and
  Jimmy Jones. "The Race Relations Competence Work-
  shop: Theory and Results." *Human Relations,* 1992. In
  Press.

This paper describes a three-day race-relations workshop
and the process used to evaluate its impact. The workshop and
its evaluation are based on embedded intergroup-relations
theory and are part of a larger organization-wide effort to
improve race relations at the fictitiously named XYZ Corporation. The evaluation is limited to employees' perceptions of the
workshop's effectiveness and race-relations issues, but the
techniques may be useful in a broader assessment.

The workshop combines experiential-learning activities
with lectures and discussion to develop race-relations competence, or "the understanding and behavior expected of black
and white managers who operate in a racially effective manner
within XYZ." The goal of the evaluation was to "determine
whether participants differed from nonparticipants in their
perceptions of race relations in the XYZ Corporation and, if so,
whether those differences had favorable or unfavorable effects
on race relations in the corporation."

Participants were surveyed four weeks after attending a
workshop about their perceptions at which time they suggested
changes in the program design. Also, a survey done after the
program had run for five years provides long-term data comparing perceptions of participants and nonparticipants. The
research team found that participants reacted favorably to the
workshop. They found that black managers evaluated the
workshop more favorably than whites, and related to that,
people having more information about the workshop rated it
more favorably.

The authors also found that workshop participants became more aware of how whites hurt blacks and "less concerned that efforts to increase racial equity meant that blacks
hurt whites." Resistance to change by some groups of first-level
managers was also analyzed.

This article, which is very technical in places, offers ideas
about how to measure the effect of a program on perceptions or
attitudes which that program is attempting to change. This
evaluation goes beyond the end-of-program ratings that are

typically the only tool used, and it encourages thinking about additional factors that might be included. A related article by Alderfer and his colleagues, which is described under the "Accountability" section of Step 3, page 89, also includes some ideas for evaluating diversity activities.

Bracken, David W. "Benchmarking Employee Attitudes." *Training & Development,* June 1992, pp. 49-52.

This is an analysis of options available to companies that wish to gauge their employees' attitudes and compare them to attitudes in organizations they admire. The three options described, from most to least desirable, are: (1) benchmark against your own company using the survey to communicate your goals, values, and priorities for improvement; (2) create a consortium with carefully selected organizations; and (3) find and use a good normative database. The benefits and drawbacks of these options are discussed, along with ways to eliminate some typical problems.

Bracken defines benchmarking as a "systematic process for comparing some aspect of an organization against that of a company that is considered to be superior in that area." This process requires a company to define its critical operations, identify companies that perform these operations exceptionally well, and collect measures at these companies and its own operations.

Step 4

Problems can arise when comparing one organization to another. For example, scales used on employee surveys sometimes differ. Also, "favorability" indices are sometimes created by combining responses into a single score (such as all the "agree" and "strongly agree" responses into a "favorable" category), which can cloud issues. Norms can be particularly troublesome because they are inherently inconsistent with benchmarking—norms present data for an "average" company, rather than an "outstanding" company. One could norm from selected "outstanding" companies by defining which companies are excellent or outstanding in the critical operations and aspects of organizational performance that are being investigated. That might involve taking data from a norm base that permits customization, or creating a consortium with carefully chosen companies.

The author notes that to choose a good normative database, you must examine the survey items used, the data submission procedures, whether the data are current (usually within the last two years), the organizations included, whether the data from these organizations is representative of the entire company, whether equal weight is given to all of the companies' responses, whether the database can be broken out by industry or demographics, and whether information is provided about the companies that are included. The ability to customize the database is another consideration.

Since the wording and response scales of survey questions are critical for comparisons, sample survey items are presented. Employees respond on a five-point scale from "strongly agree" to "strongly disagree" to such statements as, "Work activities are organized sensibly in this company," "Exceptional performance is rewarded in this organization," and "I have difficulty obtaining the information that I need in order to do my job."

This article offers practical tips for benchmarking. The author's preference that an organization benchmark against itself, what it can be and what it used to be in critical areas of a diversity effort, is a recommendation that will benefit many managers struggling with the measurement process.

Step 4

❖❖❖

Caudron, Shari. "Monsanto Responds to Diversity." *Personnel Journal*, November 1990, pp. 72-80.

A description of Monsanto's diversity effort, from its inception to its current status, is described in this article. The company began their efforts by surveying the employees about barriers to satisfaction. What they learned was that the corporate culture wasn't working for anyone, and they needed to initiate an overhaul. The overhaul began with workshops to create a long-range plan, a company-wide recruitment effort, and the creation of fourteen independent teams/task forces (including a team called "Eliminating Subtle Discrimination" which addresses work-force diversity issues).

From this task force, awareness training began. Examples are given of diversity-awareness training exercises such as telling group A that they are a member of a team in which one member isn't participating and telling group B the same scenario but that the nonparticipating member is Asian. The resulting solutions of the two groups are different, and create a climate in which discussions about diversity can begin.

A special subsection of this article is entitled, "The Dollars of Diversity." It gives the manager a tool for doing a cost/benefit analysis of diversity efforts. The four primary questions asked in this analysis are: (1) How much does the company spend each year on Equal Employment Opportunity Commission litigation, including attorney fees, settlements, and awards? (2) How much does the company spend annually on recruitment? (The writer assumes that fifty percent of such dollars are wasted if nontraditional applicants are screened out.) (3) What does it cost to train an employee and how many talented minorities and women have left the company during the past twelve months? Multiply training costs by the number of people who left. (4) How much does the company spend each year on in-house training? (The writer assumes that one-third of these dollars are wasted if training accommodates only the Anglo viewpoint.)

The special section on the dollars of diversity provides a manager with an additional means of evaluating the effectiveness of the programs that are implemented. For example, a cost analysis could be done at the onset, with the anticipated cost savings calculated. Then, at the completion of one goal, a new cost analysis could be done to see how much, or if, the situation has improved the bottom line. This method provides a means for evaluating the effectiveness of the programs being used. If costs go up, programs need to be changed.

Too often, programs are implemented and their results are never measured. The techniques described in this article can be used and tailored to help managers measure the effectiveness of a variety of diversity initiatives.

❖❖❖

Cox, Taylor H., and Stacy Blake. "Managing Cultural Diversity: Implications for Organizational Competitiveness." *Academy of Management Executive* 5:3, August 1991, pp. 45-54.

How can managing diversity create a competitive advantage for an organization? The business logic of managing diversity is the substance of this article, which reviews arguments and research data to support six business benefits: resource acquisition and cost (considered to be inevitable issues given the work-force demographics) along with marketing, creativity, problem-solving, and organizational flexibility.

The research documentation is most impressive for cost savings and problem-solving. Regarding cost savings, for example, the authors review data showing decreased turnover and absenteeism costs from tailoring benefits and work schedules to a diverse work force. The impact of diversity on problem-solving, research shows, is to improve the quality of group decisions, as minority views cause more alternatives to be considered and closer examination of assumptions and implications of choices.

Step 4

The authors define a "multicultural organization" as one that has six characteristics (including reciprocal acculturation and full integration of women and racioethnic minorities in the formal hierarchy and informal networks), and they recommend five key components for moving an organization toward that ideal. These components are: leadership from top management and from champions of diversity at lower levels; training in managing and valuing diversity; research to identify issues for educational programs and to identify areas where changes are needed; analysis and change of culture and management systems, which involves an in-depth culture audit and an agenda for change based on that; and follow-up to monitor, evaluate, and institutionalize changes, which may involve additional training and research. These components are generally regarded as critical in any organizational change effort, but the authors' brief comments on them add depth to this section.

This article persuasively pulls together data on the business impact of developing diversity, which is useful in setting standards for the results expected from a diversity effort. The difficulty in directly tying diversity to specific productivity outcomes is apparent, however, which makes the types of results more compelling than the extent of those results. The research may not overwhelm those who oppose diversity, even though a number of companies' cost savings and other success stories are included, but managers who are already inclined to pursue diversity will find this research summary helpful.

Geiger, Adrianne H. "Measures for Mentors." *Training & Development,* February 1992, pp. 65-67.

This article provides some ideas for developing your own evaluation tool by describing an instrument developed for a mentoring program at Douglas Aircraft, a subsidiary of McDonnell Douglas. Evaluations of the program were based on participants' job performance and career enhancement. To determine this, "mentorees" were asked to evaluate mentors on two aspects of mentoring: the best fulfilled mentor roles and the effects of their discussions.

Geiger developed the first part of the evaluation tool from mentor-role descriptions described by Leibowitz and Schlossberg ("Training Managers for Their Role in a Career Development System." *Training and Development Journal,* July 1981), who identified seven primary roles that the mentor fulfilled. The mentor should communicate, counsel, coach, advise, and advocate for the mentoree, and should also act as a broker and a referral agent. The tool is designed to determine both frequency of interaction and roles successfully played by the mentor.

Step 4

The second part of the evaluation tool examines the results of mentoring discussions on the employee's development. The mentoree is instructed to respond to different outcomes on a continuum between no impact and high impact. Outcomes range from acquiring a better understanding of how the organization works to learning about their management style and how to manage more effectively.

The value of this article is that it provides useful information on the evaluation of mentoring programs and contributes to an area where very little information exists. Some of the statements that the mentoree is instructed to respond to seem rather basic ("my mentor encouraged a two-way exchange of information . . ."), but nonetheless provide an avenue for beginning to develop a measurement tool.

Hinrichs, John R. "Commitment Ties to the Bottom Line." *Human Resource Magazine,* April 1991, pp. 77, 79-80.

This article indirectly addresses diversity issues in that it describes the cost savings and other financial benefits that managers can expect from increasing employees' commitment. The results of diversity activities can include less turnover, decreased absenteeism, and higher productivity for both nontraditional and traditional employees. The author describes how to quantify such results, to make the connection between diversity practices and the bottom line.

He also provides data on how much turnover, absenteeism, and decreased productivity cost an organization. For example, he reports that turnover may cost up to $200,000 per occurrence, with the average being $10,000. The cost of a one-day, unauthorized absence is $100 or more. Payroll costs often comprise 30% to 50% or more of a company's expenses, so savings gained from keeping employees satisfied can have a significant financial impact. Unfortunately, however, we are not told where these reported averages come from.

Cost data are used with actual data collected from an attitude survey to demonstrate how the financial impact can be calculated. "Typco," a hypothetical Fortune 50 company, provides a setting for this analysis. The employee survey data cover four performance areas: willingness to exert effort (productivity); company loyalty (turnover); coming to work (absenteeism); and caring about what they do (quality performance). If, as research has shown, 36% of the employees who respond on surveys that they will "probably leave" do leave the company, then turnover costs can be calculated from survey responses. Typco's survey results translate into a potential cost of $4.7 million over the next few years. The author's calculations also show that Typco has been losing about $4.2 million per

Step 4

year by ignoring the potential to increase workers' productivity, and that the company could save $111,000 a year in absenteeism costs by boosting employees' job satisfaction.

This technique measures costs and potential savings from doing things that positively affect workers' attitudes, something that many diversity activities aim to do. The calculations can be incorporated into the long-term results expected from a diversity effort. These figures are also useful in convincing senior executives of the bottom-line impact in attending to the feelings and overall well-being of both nontraditional and traditional employees.

Hooper, John. "Borrowing From the Best." *Human Resource Executive,* June 1992, pp. 38-40.

This article outlines a five-step process for benchmarking and counters several myths about the process such as, "Benchmarking won't increase my competitiveness. It's simply copying others and catching up." It familiarizes managers with a measurement tool that is increasingly being used as part of diversity initiatives. Hooper was a collaborator in the "Benchmarking HR" study described under Step 3, page 54.

Hooper suggests five basic steps to effectively benchmark.   *Step 4*
Step one, the planning stage, includes aligning improvement efforts with business goals, getting senior-management sponsorship and resources to complete the project, and creating a project team which includes functional experts, dedicated analysts, and line managers. The second step involves assessing current policies and practices and identifying key areas for improvement. Employees' attitudes, business requirements, and the extent to which current policies and practices support the company's mission, goals, and strategies also need to be considered.

Step three involves choosing the key functions and activities to benchmark, based on their impact on competitive performance, their need for improvement, and the extent to which they affect expenses. The benchmarking itself should be on companies that "are successful competitors; are diverse; have the best bottom-line performance; can demonstrate their practices promote employee satisfaction; and demonstrate the use of total-quality management principles in their practices."

The last two steps are making change recommendations and developing an action plan. The author claims that simply copying others' programs is usually not a good strategy, because they will probably be innovating while you are trying to catch up. Using ideas that will help leapfrog you ahead of competitors is a better strategy. Other advice is to start with actions that can be taken immediately to significantly improve existing practices, establish clear timelines and measurements of success, and use short-term successes to build your case for even greater improvement.

This article briefly outlines a practical process for using benchmarking as an effective measurement tool. The steps outlined by Hooper provide a useful structure for measuring the effectiveness of your diversity programs. It also takes some of the mystery out of benchmarking, which should encourage more and better use by managers.

Schaffer, Robert H., and Harvey A. Thomson. "Successful
    Change Programs Begin with Results." *Harvard Business
    Review,* January-February 1992, pp. 80-89.

Step 4

These authors argue that activity-centered change programs have about "as much impact on company performance as a rain dance has on the weather." The alternative is "results-driven improvement processes that focus on achieving specific, measurable operational improvements within a few months." The latter, they argue, often produce dramatic change and provide a learning tool for creating additional future change. Although these authors do not address diversity efforts in particular, their recommendations should be considered to make diversity initiatives more sensitive to outcomes.

Six reasons are given for the failure of many activity-centered programs: They are not keyed to specific results; they are usually too large scale and diffuse, such that the effect of any given activity cannot be determined; managers shy away from demanding short-term results for fear of undermining long-term objectives; promoters naively equate measures of activities with actual improvements in performance; programs are usually run by staff specialists or consultants instead of by operating managers; and basing programs on faith instead of evidence makes it difficult to learn useful lessons.

A results-driven approach has four key benefits that activity-centered programs generally miss: Companies must prioritize and introduce managerial and process innovations only as they are needed; empirical testing reveals what works; frequent reinforcement energizes the improvement process as short-term, incremental projects yield tangible results; and management creates a continuous learning process by building on the lessons of previous phases in designing the next phase of the program.

The authors list four guidelines for managers to get started in results-driven programs: Ask each unit to set and achieve a few ambitious short-term performance goals; periodically review progress, capture the essential learning, and reformulate strategy; institutionalize the changes that work and discard the rest; and create the context and identify the crucial business challenges.

The authors use brief case studies to illustrate their points, in which a variety of organizational problems are addressed. They are enthusiastic about results-driven programs, and provide many ideas about how to identify and measure results. It may be difficult for some practitioners, however, to relate the problem of improving thermal efficiency to one of eliminating prejudice. Many will be uncomfortable attempting a short-term, sequential approach to diversity, but the principles advocated are potentially valuable and warrant consideration in a diversity effort.

Step 4

Step 5...

USE BUILDING BLOCKS
TO MAINTAIN MOMENTUM

The impact of contextual elements and the sequencing of events in a diversity effort may explain why there is little consistency in the mix of practices used by model organizations and little agreement about which practices are effective. Building a diversity effort may be most effective when an organization's unique culture, history, and needs are taken into account. In many success stories, the pieces build upon others like building blocks, with achievements being used to drive additional activities for continued momentum.

Many organizations engaged in a diversity effort are concerned with issues regarding sex and ethnicity, and also with issues that relate to other forms of diversity. They want to apply their knowledge about domestic diversity to global or cross-national diversity, for example, or to better incorporate people who are different with respect to lifestyle or values in general. For these organizations, building diversity on diversity is an important goal, even though they begin by addressing only some forms of diversity.

This step explores the relation between diversity of sex or ethnicity and diversity of other forms. References describe the challenges of preparing managers for international assignments, an important aspect of global competitiveness. These references also cover practices to accommodate the workers of today, who consist of dual-career parents, ambitious managers unexpectedly plateaued by restructuring and brutal economics, and others who don't conform to a traditional image.

Step 5

Cross-national Issues

Adler, Nancy J. *International Dimensions of Organizational Behavior (Second Edition).* Boston: PWS-KENT, 1991. 313 pages.

This book is meant to break down barriers that limit our ability to understand and manage people throughout the world. It is divided into three parts. The first part examines the impact of culture on organizations—how cultures vary, their impact, and how to recognize the variations. The second part addresses managing cultural diversity, including cross-cultural problem solving, cross-national issues in leadership and motivation, and various approaches to negotiating. The third part focuses on managing global managers—the human resource issues in managing employees' careers and lifestyles as they move across national boundaries.

In the first part, Adler covers the four phases of international corporate evolution (domestic, international, multinational, and global) and their effect on how the business operates. She also outlines the six dimensions that describe the cultural orientations of societies, contrasting the American culture with others with respect to people's relationship to nature, space, time, other people, etc. She includes a section on how to understand someone who does not speak the same language.

The second part covers both the advantages and disadvantages of cultural and group diversity and the conditions under which diverse teams will be more effective. Adler describes the impact of diversity on three types of organizations: parochial, ethnocentric, and synergistic. The chapter on international negotiating styles, stages, and tactics includes specific recommendations and examples.

The third part focuses on the transitions that take place during employees' entry (and their spouses' as well) into another culture and their reentry, with implications for managing these transitions. Since the average cost of repatriating an executive and the family is more than $100,000, this information, and her list of selected readings on selection and training, can help organizations save considerable expense. Adler also

Step 5

reports reasons given by MBA students for accepting or rejecting an international assignment.

This book covers many useful topics related to cultural diversity that relate to business goals. Short and more extensive examples are woven throughout the book to highlight how cultural diversity can help or hurt businesses. Specific country-to-country comparisons are helpful, as are the questions for reflection that appear at the end of chapters. This book contains much information that can be used in various ways to develop cross-national diversity and to help managers better understand the diversity within their own countries.

Galagan, Patricia A. "Executive Development in a Changing
     World." *Training and Development Journal,* June 1990,
     pp. 23-35.

This article summarizes a symposium titled "Strategic Approaches to Executive Development" (sponsored by the American Society for Training and Development in October 1989), in which thirty-five experts from corporations, universities, and consulting groups discussed the new skills and competencies that executives need to become "global" executives and what changes are needed in executive development. The author maintains that the characteristics of executives prepared to handle global diversity are important in themselves and as they relate to developing the diversity within their own countries. Changes called for in this article may also be effective in a domestic diversity effort.

The experts at this symposium agreed that there is no blueprint for future executives, but they did compare some current executive traits with those needed in the future. The "all knowing" executive, for example, must move to a "leader as learner," who is more self-aware and comfortable with ambiguity. Americans are often out-learned by others partly because they learn little from their returning expatriate managers. Executives must also change from predicting the future from the past to intuiting the future. Learning from experience may not carry across geographical or cultural boundaries when executives rely solely on domestic frameworks. Future execu-

Step 5

tives must also become part of an executive team (vs. "alone at the top"), accept the paradox of order amid chaos (vs. valuing order), and inspire the trust of owners, customers, and employees (vs. boards and shareholders), among other characteristics.

Skills that these experts feel executives need to learn are: skills for understanding global business opportunities; skills for setting an organization's direction; skills for creating and implementing vision, mission, and purpose; and skills for personal understanding and effectiveness. No model currently exists for instilling these qualities into executives, but these experts emphasized that teaching these skills is a new responsibility of human resource managers.

They recommended several practices, in addition to formal training, to expand executives' thinking into global terms: rotating junior-level vice-presidents in global assignments; including younger employees in cross-national task forces; sending executives to visit key competitors in other countries; sending executives to study foreign companies in the U.S.; teaching foreign languages on a just-in-time basis; offering re-entry programs for executives returning from foreign assignments; and worldwide electronic study groups. Exposure and training such as this could be effective in developing many forms of diversity.

Developing competencies for cross-national situations is important in itself, but such competencies may also help managers more effectively deal with differences such as sex and ethnicity, both globally and domestically. Ideas for exposure and training described in this article should be considered in any organization's effort to develop diversity.

Step 5

Jelinek, Mariann, and Nancy J. Adler. "Women: World-Class Managers for Global Competition." *Academy of Management Executive* 2, February 1988, pp. 7-19.

This article emphasizes that global competitiveness demands "sophisticated, multiculturally adept managers" who use skills traditionally associated with women—"relationship development, communication, and social sensitivity across cultural differences." The authors counter the commonly-held belief that women are not prepared for international assignments by presenting evidence to the contrary from Adler's four-part study of expatriate managers.

The first part of Adler's study is a survey of 686 Canadian and U.S. firms to determine the number of women sent abroad, revealing that "of 13,338 expatriates, 402 or 3% were female." The second part of the study addresses this question in a survey of 1,129 graduating MBA students from seven U.S., Canadian, and European management schools. Overall, 84% said they'd like to go abroad at some point in their career, and there were no significant differences between women and men. The third part of the study investigates whether the low percentage of female expatriates was due to the reluctance of managers to post women overseas. Of 60 major North American multinationals, managers in 54% said they were hesitant to send women overseas. Prejudice against women was the most frequent reason cited.

The fourth part of the study addresses prejudice and other factors of success in interviews with 52 female expatriate managers while they were on assignment in Asia or shortly after their return to North America. The results show that "local women's experience is not a good predictor of North American women's reception, experiences, or success in Pacific Rim countries." What can be a predictor of their experiences, however, is managers' reluctance to commit to women sent abroad. If foreign clients detect hesitancy by the employer (for example, if a woman is only sent as a temporary solution), a self-fulfilling prophecy is often created in which the woman is expected to fail.

Nearly all of the women interviewed (97%) describe their experiences as successful, despite their companies' reluctance to expatriate women. Many of these women report that being female served more as an advantage (42%) than a disadvantage. Others said being a woman had no effect (22%) or had both advantageous and disadvantageous effects (16%). The advantages mentioned include: being very visible (foreign clients were curious about them, wanted to meet them, and remembered them well after their first meeting); having good interpersonal skills and having men open up more easily to them; and receiving special treatment as expatriates ("Asians tended to assume that the women would not have been sent

Step 5

unless they were the best"). Because the problems these women faced were most often with their home companies rather than their Asian clients, the authors encourage North American managers to set their stereotypes aside so that companies' best resources can be deployed in the global market.

Research such as this demonstrates that many of the beliefs about women in overseas assignments are indeed false. This article helps educate managers about barriers which prevent the utilization of women as expatriates in particular and, in general, the negative impact of prejudice on women and their organizations.

Johnston, William B. "Global Work Force 2000: The New World Labor Market." *Harvard Business Review,* March-April 1991, pp. 115-127.

Johnston, who directed the project reported in the 1987 book, *Workforce 2000* (Hudson Institute, June 1987), describes trends in the worldwide work force that will accelerate and otherwise affect movement of workers across national borders in "the globalization of labor." He argues that developed countries that seek foreign workers will become stronger, and that personnel policies and practices will become more standardized as some national differences among workers fade. This article highlights the need for organizations to better incorporate skilled workers from other countries.

Much of Johnston's supporting data compares work-force trends in the developed countries (Australia, Canada, France, Germany, Italy, Japan, Spain, Sweden, U.K., and U.S.) with those in developing countries (Brazil, China, India, Indonesia, Mexico, Pakistan, Philippines, South Korea, Thailand, and Turkey). He shows that the vast majority of the worldwide-labor-force growth is occurring in the developing countries, and the increase in female workers there "is an often overlooked demographic reality of industrialization" that will affect personnel policies. He also points out that the younger work force that exists in the developing nations is more recently educated and more adaptable, which may pose a competitive advantage over the developed countries.

Step 5

The statistics on education are also compelling for organizations that require skilled workers. By the year 2000, students from developing nations will comprise 60% of all college enrollees and 79% of all high-school enrollees worldwide. Further, American high-school students' performance on standardized science tests is below that in about a dozen other countries, including four developing nations.

Johnston supports free movement across national boundaries and explains how liberal immigration and emigration policies can help all nations. His political arguments may not be convincing to all managers, but the data he presents are another reminder that, in this global age, diversity can have a significant payoff for business.

Issues for Today's Workers

Hymowitz, Carol. "Stepping Off the Fast Track." *The Wall Street Journal,* June 13, 1989, p. B1.

Baby-boomer men in their thirties and early forties are demanding more leeway from their employers so they can pursue a balanced lifestyle that includes time with family and friends and leisure. This article gives a few examples of men who put their careers in perspective after the workaholic lifestyle failed to meet their needs. They, like many women who have traditionally been caught in work-family conflicts, want their employers to support their transition from a seventy-hour-a-week fast track to "the sanity track."

Step 5

Hymowitz makes the point through her interviews with high-powered executive male drop-outs that current conditions—"ferocious competition for promotions, grueling hours and, frequently, attendant family neglect"—are prompting high-potential men to opt out. Their employers' demands, which have limited the career potential of many women responsible for family care, are now increasingly likely to affect men as well. Her article provides no guidance to employers for quelling the drop-out rate, except that flexibility, often considered a "women's issue," may be the solution to a problem that affects both male and female managers.

Weber, Joseph, Lisa Driscoll, Richard Brandt, and bureau reports. "Farewell Fastrack: Promotions and Raises are Scarcer—So What Will Energize Managers?" *Business Week,* December 10, 1990, pp. 192-200.

The eighty-one million baby boomers, the recession, and work-force slashes in many organizations translate into fewer promotions and traditional incentives for high-potential managers. But the authors of this article suggest new practices to keep talented, ambitious managers loyal and stimulated.

The principles of "How to Keep Managers Motivated" include: Offer lateral movement when promotions are not available; tie raises to performance rather than seniority or title; give managers more responsibility and control; allow managers (such as "family-cherishing managers") to turn down promotions or transfers; offer managers overseas assignments; provide midcareer breaks (to attend business school, etc.); and give managers more autonomy via entrepreneurial ventures.

Examples and mini-cases help explain how these options are being used by well-established companies like DuPont, General Electric Co., Hyatt Corp., Intel Corp., Merck & Co., Inc., and Pepsico, Inc. Also, a description of the free-form management structure at W.L. Gore & Associates (maker of Gore-Tex) covers practices concerning titles (everyone is an "associate"), office space (allocated by need), pay-setting (includes associates' rankings of peers), and others.

Such new practices are needed to keep talented, ambitious managers loyal and stimulated. They also help eliminate problems created by the old fast-track system. More lateral moves, for example, have given managers a more than shallow understanding of how the company works. More time in each position allows managers to see the results of their decisions before being transferred to a new post. These experimental new approaches to development and rewards may be prompted by poor economic conditions, but they may represent useful tools in developing diversity as well.

Step 5

Executives forced into finding ways to motivate and challenge their middle managers on the new "Slow Track" may find the ideas in this article useful in developing nontraditional as well as traditional managers during slow-growth periods.

Step 5

General References

Gen
Refs

A BNA Special Report: Promoting Minorities & Women.
    A Practical Guide to Affirmative Action for the 1990s.
    Washington, D.C.: The Bureau of National Affairs, Inc.
    1989. 338 pages.

This report provides background on EEO/AA (Equal
Employment Opportunity/Affirmative Action) programs, describes six case studies of effective diversity programs (Gannett
Co., Inc., U.S. West, Inc., Aetna Life & Casualty Co., Xerox
Corporation, AT&T, and The Chase Manhattan Bank, N.A.),
and shows thorough analysis of the legal environment and
historical context, both how far we've come and how far we
have to go in terms of equal opportunity.
        In one chapter of the book, several EEOC officials were
surveyed and interviewed about the federal government's role
in advancing women and people of color, barriers which continue to exist which limit their advancement, and how to best
design and implement policies aimed at advancing women and
people of color. Most officials agreed that the federal government should exert more pressure on organizations to advance
these groups. One of their recommendations was to tie progress
on diversity to managers' pay raises, promotions, and bonuses.
        In a contributed chapter, Ed Jones (President of Corpo-
rate Organizational Dynamics, Inc. of South Orange, NJ)
suggests ways of fully utilizing highly trained people of color.
He counters the popular argument that top executives "can't
find qualified people of color" by noting that "more education is
the solution only if the most highly educated are succeeding."
He argues that managers must learn inclusive organizational
behaviors, that equal opportunity must be identified as a
strategic business issue, and that managers must learn to
recognize the value in the differing experiences of people of
color and women.
        The case studies provide ideas about how to develop
diversity in organizations. Gannett actively monitors its efforts
and holds managers accountable for progress by tying progress
to their bonuses. U.S. West has an intensive training program
to prepare women of color for management positions. Aetna
uses a program called the "Consulting Pairs" which pairs up
employees of different racial or ethnic backgrounds to address
diversity issues. Xerox offers training programs to its managers

to examine work-force diversity issues. There are also more than one hundred support groups to address the concerns of women and people of color. AT&T allows employees to serve as visiting professors at historically black universities in an effort to recruit more people of color. Internships are also offered at Bell Labs for students of color. Chase Manhattan sponsors a summer internship program that includes students of color in business training classes with entry-level, full-time employees.

Appendix C shows the actual corporate promotion plans used at Gannett, Xerox, and Aetna. Appendix D gives examples of surveys used by BNA, Sirota Alper & Pfau, and Korn/Ferry International. Stressing a legal/governmental orientation to diversity, this report may complement other works, but may be partly dated since the 1991 Civil Rights Bill. The case studies, sample forms and questionnaires in the appendix, and other content, however, reveal important, practical lessons for any diversity effort. These include: Get top-level commitment; measure and enforce results; communicate a business rationale; and counter the "old boy network."

Fernandez, John P. *Managing a Diverse Work Force: Regaining the Competitive Edge.* Lexington, MA: Lexington Books, 1991. 322 pages.

In his most recent book, Fernandez emphasizes the business imperative of developing diversity in organizations to give the U.S. a needed competitive advantage over Japan and the European Community. He appeals to senior management: "The United States is best positioned to take advantage of its diversity. We have the right philosophy, we have the legal foundation, but we need the proactive personal commitment."

Fernandez' 1988-89 survey data and previous data from more than 50,000 employees are incorporated in this book. Some of the data and even entire sections of this book are repeated from earlier books (two of which are described under Step 1, page 22), but this book is distinctive because it takes a broader view of diversity. It covers cross-national issues related to global economics; issues pertinent to various specific groups of people of color within the U.S.; and aspects of difference

Gen Refs

other than sex and ethnicity, such as age and various degrees of physical challenge. Charts showing survey data and comments made by the respondents illustrate his points throughout the text.

Fernandez argues that Japan will not be as economically competitive in the future "because of Japan's inability to change rapidly its racist, sexist, ethnocentric, and xenophobic culture" and that Japan's treatment of racial minorities and women is comparable to what occurred in the U.S. in the 1930s. He also argues that Europe, while advancing their economies dramatically by reducing trade barriers, has not been able to effectively manage issues of race, ethnicity, religious differences, language, culture, and gender. He compares Europe's treatment of women and people of color to that in the U.S. during the late 1950s and early 1960s. His arguments are intended to convince managers to use the potential U.S. workforce advantage for business success.

Each of a number of diverse groups that comprise the U.S. work force are analyzed—women, Native Americans, Asian-Americans, blacks, and Hispanics—in terms of their history, the nature of discrimination against them, and perceptions by and about them in the workplace. A chapter is also devoted to diversity issues of age, religion, sexual preference, and the disabled, which covers demographic changes, laws, and changing views. Much of the rest of the book is information from previous works that has been repackaged or repeated here, including sections on the dysfunctional effect of bureaucracies, strategies for success for nontraditional managers, and seven "realities" in response to white-male managers' backlash.

As in earlier works, Fernandez' advice for organization-level change is limited. He suggests ways to "minimize bureaucratic structural and policy issues" through feedback to employees, training in communication, better tools for evaluating subordinates' performance and potential, and so on, but his recommendations lack detail. The strength of this book is that it ties diversity to competitive advantage in the global marketplace, a link which may gain support among business executives.

❖❖❖

Morrison, Ann M. *The New Leaders: Guidelines on Leadership Diversity in America.* San Francisco: Jossey-Bass Inc., 1992. 317 pages.

This book provides the framework for this digest. The five steps and sections into which the digest is organized come from the action process recommended in *The New Leaders.* Based on a three-year study of sixteen model organizations, the book addresses several questions important to managers in carrying out a diversity effort: What barriers currently exist which limit the advancement of white women and people of color into executive levels? What programs and practices are progressive organizations using to counter these barriers? Which key ingredients contribute to the success or failure of diversity practices? How should an organization undertake a diversity effort to have the best chance of success?

The book is divided into three parts. The first part discusses the benefits and challenges cited by nearly two hundred managers and executives interviewed who are involved in incorporating diversity into the business agenda. It covers the advantages of implementing diversity programs, and discusses the types and extent of differential treatment that still occurs in the workplace based on sex and ethnicity. Also, this part highlights the importance of incorporating the elements of challenge, recognition, and support in the practices designed to develop the leadership potential of nontraditional managers.

The second part covers the three types of practices (development, accountability, and recruitment) available to develop diversity. These practices support a three-fold strategic approach that includes education, enforcement, and exposure. Detailed descriptions and examples of the most important practices are offered, including an analysis of their strengths and liabilities. The fifty-two types of practices include interventions by top management, employee advocacy groups, hiring in key executives, diversity-awareness training, and monitoring statistical goals.

The third part lays out an action plan that can be tailored to an organization's specific context. The five action steps, described in detail, incorporate basic principles of organizational change which are often ignored in diversity efforts because of the sensitivity and emotional nature of the issues.

Gen
Refs

The five steps are: (1) Discover (and rediscover) the problems in your organization; (2) strengthen top-management commitment; (3) choose solutions that fit a balanced strategy; (4) demand results and revisit goals; and (5) use building blocks to maintain momentum. A chapter is dedicated to each step, and specific guidelines are listed within each step.

This work goes beyond many other references in providing detailed information about specific tools and techniques used in diversity efforts. It is useful in that it compares activities across organizations to identify patterns that can help other organizations—regardless of size, sector, location, or industry— effectively pursue a diversity agenda. It provides a framework that is flexible enough for managers to use to arrive at their own "best practices."

Powell, Gary N. *Women & Men in Management.* Newbury Park, CA: Sage Publications, 1988. 260 pages.

Although more women are in management positions now than in the 1970s, women's representation in top-management positions has not increased proportionally. Why this is, and what individuals and organizations can do about it, is the thesis of this book.

An historical account of the socialization of women and men provides a basis for understanding why gender-based stereotypes persevere. Powell compares research-identified sex differences with stereotypes, examines biases in hiring decisions (both the applicant's and the organization's), describes the effects of gender stereotypes on men's and women's work relationships, analyzes leadership and manager-style differences (determining that stereotypes which advocate that men are more effective managers are inaccurate), reviews laws which have been enacted to promote equal opportunity for women in organizations, and recommends ways organizations can best promote equal opportunity.

His chapter on "Getting ahead" analyzes career-development models and theories. Although Powell does not devise a career-development strategy, he does suggest that several factors should be included in such a theory (e.g, societal

Gen Refs

factors, organizational practices, personal factors, and family factors), and he critiques and analyzes early and current career-development theories.

Powell concludes his book by offering two possible future scenarios for women and men in organizations, and he discusses the factors that could potentially shape the future. These factors include: the extent to which the proportion of female managers will continue to increase, the management style that will predominate, the extent to which traditional norms about women's and men's roles will disappear, changes to EEOC (Equal Employment Opportunity Commission) laws, the extent to which sex differences in socialization experiences will disappear, and whether women's and men's careers are equally affected by family concerns.

The chapters open with interesting scenarios, poems, or quotations to help introduce the issues, which makes the material more enjoyable to read. This is a thorough and thoughtful account of women in organizations—their history, their current status, and their possible future—and a resource for practitioners interested in a career-development model for women. Also, Powell's review of career-development models and theories is extensive, and it could contribute to shaping a new career-development model appropriate for women.

Smith, Mary Ann, and Sandra J. Johnson, eds. *Valuing Differences in the Workplace: Theory-to-Practice Monograph Series.* Alexandria, VA: American Society for Training and Development, 1991. 181 pages.

This report is the outcome of a symposium sponsored by ASTD's Research Committee and the University of Minnesota's Training and Development Research Center. It was inspired by Barbara Walker's Valuing Differences project at Digital Equipment Corp. Walker's conceptual model serves as the foundation on which a number of other authors build—they address the theory behind this model, its history, and ways to make a valuing differences approach work in an organization.

The model is based on four key principles: People work best when they feel valued; people feel most valued when they

Gen Refs

believe that their individual and group differences have been taken into account; the ability to learn from people regarded as different is the key to becoming fully empowered; when people feel valued and empowered, they are able to build interdependent and synergistic relationships. The author also details five steps in the process of valuing differences: Strip away stereotypes; learn to listen and probe for the differences in people's assumptions; build authentic and significant relationships with people one regards as different; enhance personal empowerment; and explore and identify group differences.

Section 1 begins with Walker's description of a small core group at Digital and how Digital worked to capitalize on the diverse work force. Other authors in this section support her model with theoretical perspectives. Section 2 recounts the history behind attempts to achieve equality in the work force. Section 3 provides methods for assessing an organization's readiness to adopt a valuing diversity program. Section 4 briefly describes six different diversity efforts: Digital (Walker); Digital-Springfield; University of Massachusetts-Amherst; Ford Motor Company; 3M; and Mendez Russell Training and Development.

Because this work incorporates the views of practitioners and academics, it provides a well-rounded perspective on building and carrying out the vision of valuing differences.

Thompson, Donna E., and Nancy DiTomaso, eds. *Ensuring Minority Success in Corporate Management.* New York: Plenum Press, 1988. 387 pages.

This book is based on a conference (sponsored by Rutgers Graduate School of Management in September 1984) designed to facilitate communication between academics and executives about people of color in management. It discusses why so few people of color exist and succeed in top corporate-management positions and how corporations and management schools can improve their chances of success in the future. The book is very action-oriented in that its goal is to take the practitioner beyond the necessary first step of identifying the problem to the step of finding a solution. The editors focus on three steps: how organizations learn to gather facts and information about critical issues, problems, and concerns about the immobility of people of color; how they should generate solutions; and how to develop plans of action.

The book covers issues such as the current status of people of color in management, ways that managers of color have successfully overcome or coped with barriers to advancement, employee attitude survey methods, and techniques to assess problems and needs. A history of racism and sexism in corporate America sheds light on why current problems exist and how to recognize them. A chapter by John Fernandez (whose books are discussed in Step 1, page 22, and General References, page 115), for example, provides a "then and now" analysis of racism and sexism in corporations. In another section, ten successful managers of color reflect on their organizational experiences and advise other people of color based on what they feel they did right and wrong as they advanced in their careers.

Authors also describe practices that have worked in their companies, and they give recommendations for action. Eight case studies by human resource managers reveal what their corporations do to successfully manage the diverse work force. For example, Allied-Signal ties senior managers' compensation to the accomplishment of equal opportunity goals. Other companies described include Bank of America, Merck & Co., Inc., AT&T, and McNeil Pharmaceutical. The editors and a colleague include their overview of corporate policies and practices and the action steps they recommend for companies and graduate business schools, which are based on survey data from two-hundred eighteen corporate CEOs. They found that the most commonly used diversity programs were feedback, goal-setting, and training, and that the least frequently used program was mentoring. Results from their survey also suggest that some programs relate to the successful promotion of people of color to middle management while others relate mainly to upper management.

Gen Refs

This book is helpful for anyone designing activities to help people of color advance. The concepts and techniques revealed in each section will help practitioners develop a meaningful plan of action for their organizations. Because it is an edited volume written by a variety of authors with different perspectives, it is very useful for understanding the problems and deciding what to do about them. Almost every chapter has penetrating insights or suggestions for concrete tools to incorporate into a diversity effort.

Case Studies

Jackson, Susan E., and Associates. *Diversity in the Workplace: Human Resources Initiatives.* New York: The Guilford Press, 1992. 356 pages.

This book provides three case studies for each of three important methods of developing the diverse work force: creating and assessing the diverse workplace; using personal growth and team development; and using strategic initiatives. The cases and the chapters analyzing diversity issues were written by human resource professionals and consultants as well as academics.

The section on how to create and assess the diverse workplace includes initiatives aimed at recruiting new (diverse) hires, establishing new rules of organizational operation, and evaluating the productivity, creativity, and effectiveness of employees in the organization. The Xerox Corp. case study demonstrates the balance needed between short-term diversity goals (caucus groups) and long-term goals exemplified by their Balanced Work Force goal initiative. Pacific Bell focused on Hispanic recruitment and went far beyond traditional methods. Instead of merely attracting the most qualified people of color, Pacific Bell worked to increase the number of qualified applicants through workshops on job hunting, and through fellowships and internships. These programs were continually monitored and evaluated. The federal government's "Quality Assessment Program" includes data from more than 160,000 job applicants and compares them to the private-sector work force.

In the section on using personal growth and team development, case studies describe education programs and group discussions designed to change attitudes and behavior toward those who are similar and dissimilar to oneself. At Digital

Equipment Corp., Core Group leaders recognized that whenever people discussed differences, "the emotional decibel level would skyrocket"; the phrase "keep people safe" became a code to help make the Core Groups work. Clayton Alderfer's chapter on the long-term process used to change race relations in the so-called XYZ Corporation (Section 3, page 89) incorporates a theoretical framework concerning embedded groups. The merger of Harris Semiconductors and General Electric Solid State compares issues of demographic diversity to those of integrating two separate corporate cultures.

Strategic initiatives (long-term efforts intentionally planned and targeted toward business objectives which involve the entire organization) are described in cases about American Express Travel Related Services, Coopers & Lybrand, and Pepsi-Cola International. Coopers & Lybrand executives, for example, ensure that work-force diversity goals will be accomplished by positioning these in parallel to other types of diversity such as that in their markets, products, and services.

While cases do not provide a recipe for taking action, this book provides detail and insight to help managers focus on important concepts and techniques in developing diversity. Jackson and her colleagues synthesize information from the cases, highlight key issues and recurrent themes, offer commentary about approaches used in these organizations, and describe dilemmas related to diversity aims, activities and strategies. They also apply principles of organizational change to working through diversity issues. These analyses and the detailed case examples can stimulate ideas for practitioners.

❖❖❖

Thomas, Roosevelt R., Jr., Tracy Irving Gray, Jr., and Marjorie Woodroof. *Differences Do Make a Difference.* Atlanta: The American Institute for Managing Diversity, 1992. 155 pages.

Through use of case studies of thirteen mid- and high-level employees, Thomas and his colleagues paint a picture of the decreasing productivity that results when the diverse work force is not fully utilized. Examples of employees' disillusionment, decreased motivation, and transfer of their energy to outside the corporation demonstrate that loss of productivity.

The life stories that comprise most of this book provide a look at the personalities behind the statistics of the changing work force. The thirteen cases, based on interviews across the country, are in three sections: those willing to leave; those who stay and stay mad; and those who continue to debate the issues. Some high-potential, well-educated and extensively trained employees choose to leave their organizations to either start their own businesses or join other firms that seem to offer more opportunities for advancement. Other employees choose to stay in their present organizations but limit their association as they seek gratification in community work. Still others are satisfied with their jobs and the rewards and recognition they have received, but they perceive limits on their advancement or potential contribution.

Several themes run through these stories. Mentors, for example, are frequently linked with advancement. Cynicism is experienced by a number of people of color and women who feel excluded from the executive circle. People who are "different" operate under a microscope in which every aspect of their performance is judged hypercritically, and any mistake is easily blown out of proportion.

Thomas and his colleagues criticize traditional diversity-related initiatives which have "defined healthy white males as the norm, all others as diverse" because this idea equates "diverse" with "less than" and doesn't recognize that white men make up part of the diversity package. They also argue that organizations must examine their rules and cultural assumptions and decide which of these are essential to achieve the organization's objectives, which prevent full productivity, and which are not essential to the profitable operation of the business. They suggest that only the essential elements of the organizational structure be preserved; the others can and should be changed to more fully utilize the talents of the diverse work force.

This book reads quickly and might be used for training sessions or meetings to bring important diversity issues to life via examples. The stories may help organizational leaders recognize that instituting formal organizational change can regain the dedication and full productivity of workers who have become discouraged and disenchanted.

Best Companies

"25 Best Places for Blacks to Work." *Black Enterprise,*
    February 1992, pp. 71-94.

This article opens with a discussion of the impact that the Reagan and Bush administrations, and the economic conditions, have had on African-American managers. It describes the evolution of the "Best Places" list: In 1982, *Black Enterprise* magazine *(BE)* identified ten companies; in 1986, *BE* identified twenty-five companies; in 1989, the number was expanded to fifty companies, and *BE* added "fifteen companies to watch"; this year, *BE* found only twenty-five companies that exemplified the commitment and success potential of strong affirmative-action policies.

Criteria used for rating the organizations include: statistics on black employees, managers, and senior managers; information about the companies' recruitment programs for people of color; and total-dollar value of minority contracts, and minority participation in management training, development, and fast-track programs. The staff also considered how blacks are used in decision-making teams throughout the organization, their level of task assignments, and whether the companies invest in all its people with training and development programs designed to improve productivity and quality. Companies that made it onto the list are: Ameritech, AT&T, Avon Products, Inc., Chrysler Corporation, Coca-Cola, Corning Incorporated, DuPont, Equitable Life Assurance Society of the United States, Federal Express Corp., Ford Motor Co., Gannett Co., Inc., General Mills, Inc., General Motors Corp., IBM, Johnson & Johnson, Kellogg's, Marriott Corporation, McDonald's, Merck & Co., Inc., Nynex Corporation, Pepsico, Inc., Philip Morris Companies, Inc., TIAA-CREF, UAL Corporation, and Xerox Corporation. A sidebar on military management acknowledges the progress made in the army for blacks.

Gen Refs

Like other lists, this one can serve practitioners by illustrating the criteria used to judge the "fairness" of a company.
The information about various companies that have been
successful at implementing equitable programs, effective at
utilizing skills of people of color, and supportive of minority
organizations can help practitioners understand what their
task involves at their own company, and perhaps gain insight
as to how to manage the changes needed.

Estrada, Alfredo J. "1992 Hispanic 100." *Hispanic,* January-
February 1992, pp. 49-76.

This third annual listing of the Hispanic 100 recognizes
"the one hundred companies providing the most opportunities
for Hispanics." *Hispanic* magazine prepares this list to give
free publicity to the companies mentioned, since inclusion may
"serve as a stimulus for increased involvement with the
Hispanic community."

The staff of *Hispanic,* with input from people of color who
are business experts and representatives of Hispanic organizations, used survey responses from more than five hundred U.S.
corporations and four criteria to select these one hundred
companies: recruitment and hiring; scholarships and grants;
support for Hispanic organizations; and minority-vendor programs.

Some companies highlighted by the author include Philip
Morris Companies, Inc., for its long-standing tradition of
supporting Hispanics, through activities such as having executives serve on boards of Hispanic groups and supporting the
National Association of Hispanic Publications' voter
registration/participation program. General Motors Corp. is
cited for maintaining support of national and local Hispanic
organizations despite hard times in the domestic auto industry.
The author notes that "GM's minority supplier development
goals for 1991 were to spend $200 million with Hispanic ven-
dors." Lockheed Corp.'s aggressive outreach to vendors of color
is also praised. Lockheed helped found a joint effort with the
California Community Colleges to conduct total-quality management training to enable small businesses to work with

*Gen
Refs*

aerospace companies. A very brief description of each company's diversity activities is included in this article.

Estrada notes that certain industries are well-represented in the Hispanic 100, such as the automotive industry (GM, Ford Motor Co., Chrysler Corporation), high-tech and defense (Lockheed, Rockwell International, EDS Corp., and Hughes Aircraft Company), consumer companies (Pepsico, Inc., Coca-Cola, and McDonald's), and telecommunications (AT&T, Southwestern Bell, and U.S. Sprint). Other industries have little or no representation, such as cosmetics, banks and financial services, pharmaceutical companies, and large media conglomerates.

Like other "best companies" lists, the Hispanic 100 can serve practitioners by illustrating the criteria used to judge organizations as employers of nontraditionals and by providing benchmarks by which to gauge their own status. For those included on the list, the public recognition of past diversity efforts also encourages continued, expanded activities that maintain momentum.

Konrad, Walecia. "Welcome to the Woman-Friendly Company." *Business Week,* August 6, 1990, pp. 48-55.

This article gives examples of several ways companies are making themselves more woman-friendly: cutting back on required travel, relocation, and long work schedules; providing extended leaves, flextime, and eldercare assistance; tying managers' compensation to their success in meeting diversity goals; and creating a climate where women and other nontraditionals can flourish. Konrad notes that providing family benefits isn't enough to attract talented women, who also need to see good career prospects for themselves.

To identify "woman-friendly" companies, *Business Week* looked for major public corporations that met several criteria: They support the idea that at least twenty percent of top management are women, with at least one or two reporting directly to the CEO; maintain a good middle-management pipeline; encourage company efforts to help women advance; and are sensitive to work-family issues.

Gen Refs

The short list of "pacesetter" companies consists of Avon Products, Inc., Columbia Broadcasting System, Dayton-Hudson Corp., Gannett Co., Inc., Kelly Services, and U.S. West, Inc. "Up-and-coming" companies identified are: American Express, Baxter International Inc., Corning Incorporated, Honeywell Inc., IBM, Johnson & Johnson, Merck & Co., Inc., Monsanto, Pitney Bowes, Reader's Digest, Security Pacific Bank, and Square D & Co. Six "late bloomers" are: Digital Equipment Corp., DuPont, Hewlett-Packard Co., Olin Corp., 3M, and Xerox Corporation. The progress and key activities of each of these companies are noted.

A sidebar titled "Is your company woman-friendly?" offers a short, somewhat tongue-in-cheek quiz (based on *Business Week*'s selection criteria) that can be self-administered and self-scored to put a company into categories from "visionary" or "woman-friendly" to "class-action candidate" or "boss preferred the good old days." Results from a recent Harris poll on how female managers see their companies are also included in this article. The poll items can help identify issues to investigate in an internal audit, such as what obstacles women face and what existing practices encourage women. The respondents in this study, however, are rather pessimistic—about half said it would take more than ten years before their company named a female CEO, and another twenty percent said "never."

The criteria and the examples offered in this article can help organizations assess their own status and perhaps identify some areas for development.

Zeitz, Baila, and Lorraine Dusky. *The Best Companies for Women.* New York: Simon and Schuster, 1988. 413 pages.

Gen Refs

This book provides information on fifty U.S. companies that are considered to be responsive to women's needs. Factors in the selection process include: the number of employees and percentages of female employees; recruiting and hiring of women; promotion of women; number of women in upper management; number of women on the board of directors; pay and thinking on how to rectify inequality of pay; commitment to equality; how the company addresses sexual discrimination and sexual harassment; training programs on sexual harassment; flextime; flexibility for parenting needs including maternity, paternity, and adoption benefits; on-site child care; subsidies for child care; resource referral directory for child-care facilities; cafeteria-style approach to benefits; part-time work for managers and professionals; policies on employing couples; sick leave for family illness; and leave without pay, position assured.

The book is intended to help women at every stage of their careers decide which companies would be best for them to seek employment. The companies listed are: American Express/ Shearson Lehman Hutton; AT&T; Avon Products, Inc.; Barrios Technology; Bidermann Industries; Columbia Broadcasting System; Children's Television Workshop; Citizens and Southern; Cognos Inc.; Conran Stores; The Denver Post; Digital Equipment Corp.; Drake Business Schools; Federal Express Corp.; Fidelity Bank; First Atlanta; Gannett Co., Inc.; General Mills, Inc.; Grey Advertising; GTE Corporation; Hallmark Cards Inc.; Hearst Trade Books; Herman Miller, Inc.; Hewitt Associates; Hewlett-Packard Co.; Home Box Office; Honeywell Inc.; IBM; Levi Strauss; Lotus Development Corp.; Manufacturers Hanover Trust; Merck & Co., Inc.; Mountain Bell; Mount Carmel Health; Neiman-Marcus; Northwestern Bell; Payless Cashways; Pepsico, Inc.; Pitney Bowes; Procter & Gamble Co.; Recognition Equipment; Restaurant Enterprises Group; The Rowland Company; Saks Fifth Avenue; Salomon Brothers; Simon & Schuster Inc.; Southern New England Telephone; Syntex; Time Inc.; and U.S. West, Inc. The authors explain why Johnson & Johnson and Control Data Corp. were not on their list, despite their good reputations.

This work is most helpful to managers in that it defines criteria which can be used to measure the effectiveness of an organization's diversity initiative. It also provides ideas about new programs that managers might try in their own organizations. The companies listed may also be considered by managers for inclusion in a benchmarking project.

For those who prefer less detail, a short summary of this book, which includes the list of best companies, was published in *Savvy* magazine (May 1988).

Appendix

FOR THOSE WHO NEED MORE

Alderfer, Clayton. "The New Corporate Language for Race
Relations." Conference presentation at Academy of Management Meeting, 11 August 1991, Miami Beach, Florida. (203)
393-3958. 28 pages.

Cabezas, Amado. "The Asian American Today as an Economic
Success Model: Some Myths and Realities." Break the
Silence: A Conference on Anti-Asian Violence. May 10,
1986. UC Berkeley Boalt Hall Proceedings. (510) 642-2199.
6 pages.

Ehasz-Sanz, Maribeth, and Thomas F. McIlwain. "The Management Implications of Career Development Concerns of
Employed Women." Conference paper from the 1991 Academy of Management Meeting: Women in Management
Division, Miami Beach, Florida. Ehasz-Sanz at (704) 262-
2700 or McIlwain at (704) 262-6231. 12 pages.

Howard, J., and Associates, Inc. "TQHRD: Meeting the De-
mands of Total Quality Management with the Workforce
We Have Now." Lexington, MA: J. Howard and Associates,
Inc., 1991. (617) 862-8887.

Lapid-Bogda, Ginger, and Sunny Bradford. "Diverse Approaches to Diversity: What, When and Why." Lapid-Bogda
at (310) 440-9772 or Bradford (714) 949-8242. 7 pages.

Ohlott, Patricia J., Marian N. Ruderman, and Cynthia D.
McCauley. "Women and Men: Equal Opportunity For
Development?" Paper submitted to the Women in Manage-
ment Division for the Academy of Management Conference,
San Francisco, CA, August 1990. Greensboro, NC: Center
for Creative Leadership. (919) 288-7210. 20 pages.

Torres, Cresencio, and Mary Bruxelles. "Effective Diversity
Workforce Management: Break the Cycle of Disillusion-
ment." San Diego: Consultants for Change, Inc., 1991.
Torres at (619) 453-4774. 10 pages.

Index

BOOK AND ARTICLE AUTHORS

OTHER BOOKS ON DIVERSITY AVAILABLE FROM THE CENTER FOR CREATIVE LEADERSHIP

Breaking the Glass Ceiling: Can Women Reach the Top of America's Largest Corporations?
by Ann M. Morrison, Randall P. White, Ellen Van Velsor, and the Center for Creative Leadership (Updated Edition; Addison-Wesley, 1992). (No. 236R). ISBN 0-201-93214-4

Based on a three-year study of female executives, this book examines the factors that determine success or derailment in the corporate environment and shows how women can break the "glass ceiling." The updated edition includes current statistics and the latest trends in business and government for women in management and people of color.

Gender Differences in the Development of Managers: How Women Managers Learn From Experience
by Ellen Van Velsor and Martha W. Hughes (Center for Creative Leadership, 1990). (No. 145R). ISBN 0-912879-42-4

This research report provides an analysis of what career experiences women lack and describes how women's patterns of learning differ from those of men.

The New Leaders: Guidelines on Leadership Diversity in America
by Ann M. Morrison (Jossey-Bass, 1992). (No. 238R). ISBN 1-55542-459-7

This book reports on the findings of the Center for Creative Leadership's Guidelines on Leadership Diversity project, whose goal was to identify the most effective practices for advancing nontraditional managers. It identifies the "best practices" for fostering diversity and recommends five action steps for developing it in any organization.

Making Diversity Happen in Organizations
(working title)
by Ann M. Morrison, Marian N. Ruderman, and Martha Hughes-James (Center for Creative Leadership, 1993). (No. 320R). ISBN 0-912879-72-6

This book reports on and interprets discussions held at "Leadership Diversity: Beyond Awareness Into Action," a working conference sponsored by the Center in 1992. It compares and contrasts the views of researchers, corporate practitioners, and consultants on the meaning of diversity and the approaches to its implementation in organizations.

(See next page for ordering information.)

To place your order for the following publications, please copy this form, fill it out, and return to: **Publication, Center for Creative Leadership, P.O. Box 26300, Greensboro, NC 27438-6300,** or **FAX to 919-288-3999,** or **phone 919-545-2805** (after November 15, 1993, please use area code 910). All orders must be PREPAID (checks should be made payable to the Center for Creative Leadership) or charged to VISA, MasterCard, American Express, or Discover. All prices subject to change. Quantity discounts are available.

_____
NAME

_____
TITLE

_____
ORGANIZATION

_____
ADDRESS   CITY/STATE/ZIP

_____
TELEPHONE   FAX

Quantity

_____ **Developing Diversity In Organizations: A Digest of Selected Literature.** (No. 317R). **$20.00.**

_____ **Breaking the Glass Ceiling: Can Women Reach the Top of America's Largest Corporations? (Updated 1992).** (No. 236R). **$19.95.**

_____ **Gender Differences in the Development of Managers: How Women Managers Learn from Experience.** (No. 145R). **$30.00.**

_____ **The New Leaders: Guidelines on Leadership Diversity in America.** (No. 238R). **$25.95.**

_____ **Making Diversity Happen in Organizations** (working title). (No. 320R). **$20.00.**

❏ My check or money order in the amount of $_____ is enclosed.

❏ Charge my order, plus shipping, to my credit card:
    ❏ VISA   ❏ MasterCard   ❏ American Express   ❏ Discover

    Account Number _____

    Expiration Date: Mo. ____ Yr. ____

    Name of issuing bank: _____

    Signature: _____

                                    Subtotal $ _____

                  All NC Residents add 6% Sales Tax _____

    Shipping and Handling is 5% of Subtotal ($3.00 minimum) _____

                                    Total $ _____

❏ **Please send me a copy of your Resource Guide.**